Southern Lady

LUNCHEONS, TEAS
& *Holiday Celebrations*

Southern Lady
LUNCHEONS, TEAS
& Holiday Celebrations

A YEAR OF MENUS FOR THE GRACIOUS HOSTESS

hm | books

hm | books

EXECUTIVE VICE PRESIDENT/CCO Brian K. Hoffman
VICE PRESIDENT/EDITORIAL Cindy Smith Cooper
ART DIRECTOR Stephanie Lambert

SOUTHERN LADY EDITORIAL

EDITOR Andrea Fanning
CREATIVE DIRECTOR/PHOTOGRAPHY Mac Jamieson
ART DIRECTORS Amy Robinson, Jennifer Richburg,
    Karissa Brown, Jessica Stalnaker, Ann McKeand Carothers
ASSOCIATE EDITORS Karen Pruitt Callaway,
    Kathleen Johnston Whaley
ASSISTANT EDITOR K. Faith Morgan
EDITORIAL COORDINATOR Becky Goff
COPY EDITOR Nancy Ogburn
CONTRIBUTING COPY EDITOR Donna Baldone
CONTRIBUTING WRITER Heather Jeffcoat
STYLISTS Tracey M. Runnion, Katherine Tucker,
    Adrienne Alldredge Williams, Yukie McLean
SENIOR PHOTOGRAPHERS Marcy Black Simpson, John O'Hagan
PHOTOGRAPHERS William Dickey, Stephanie Welbourne Grund,
    Sarah Arrington, Kamin Williams
CONTRIBUTING PHOTOGRAPHER Kimberly Finkel Davis
TEST KITCHEN DIRECTOR Janice Ritter
EXECUTIVE CHEF Rebecca Treadwell
FOOD EDITOR Aimee Bishop Lindsey
TEST KITCHEN PROFESSIONALS Rachael Daylong, Kathleen Kanen,
    Janet Lambert, Elizabeth Nelson, Loren Wood
TEST KITCHEN ASSISTANT Anita Simpson Spain
CONTRIBUTING FOOD STYLISTS Chantel Lambeth,
    Virginia Hornbuckle
SENIOR DIGITAL IMAGING SPECIALIST Delisa McDaniel
DIGITAL IMAGING SPECIALIST Clark Densmore

hm
hoffmanmedia

PRESIDENT Phyllis Hoffman DePiano
EXECUTIVE VICE PRESIDENT/COO Eric W. Hoffman
EXECUTIVE VICE PRESIDENT/CCO Brian K. Hoffman
EXECUTIVE VICE PRESIDENT/CFO G. Marc Neas
VICE PRESIDENT/MANUFACTURING Greg Baugh
VICE PRESIDENT/EDITORIAL Cindy Smith Cooper
VICE PRESIDENT/CONSUMER MARKETING Silvia Rider
VICE PRESIDENT/ADMINISTRATION Lynn Lee Terry

Hoffman Media
1900 International Park Drive, Suite 50
Birmingham, Alabama 35243
www.hoffmanmedia.com

ISBN # 978-0-97700694-6

Printed in Mexico

On the cover: Spoonful of Sugar Teacakes, page 50.
Photography by John O'Hagan.
Recipe Development and Food styling by Aimee Bishop Lindsey.

Contents

Introduction

The ability to be a gracious hostess is a timeless craft, one that is just as important today as in the past. We learn the art of entertaining over a lifetime, taking cues from the way our grandmothers pressed the table linens and the way our mothers turned pantry staples into party-perfect dishes. With every luncheon, shower, tea, and birthday bash we host, we hone our skills a bit more and discover new ways to make the moments shine.

Southern sensibilities go hand in hand with successful soirees and shindigs, and no matter the occasion, the ultimate goal is to make each guest feel special. From handwritten place cards to monogrammed napkins and sparkling crystal to take-home treats, thoughtful details help turn an ordinary gathering into a grand event. And we all know that a party is only as good as the food served, which is why we have filled these pages with some of the best recipes from *Southern Lady* magazine. We have also included some of our favorite entertaining tips and ideas, and we hope they will serve you well as you tie your apron strings, don that stunning smile, welcome dear ones into your home, and continue the legacy of gracious Southern hospitality.

Cheers,
Southern Lady

Spring

*The daffodils and violets have shaken off their frosty
coverings and burst forth to the merry song of the
bluebirds. New life and new blooms signal the start of this,
the most colorful of seasons.*

Easter

Easter
TIDINGS

·

Adults and children alike love the arrival of spring because with it comes beautiful blooming flowers, days of frolicking outdoors in the warm sun, and best of all—Easter! Spend a day during this renewed season hosting an Easter lunch full of wonderful savory flavors and ending with a special confection.

MENU

SPINACH AND MUSHROOM
STUFFED PORK LOIN WITH
LEMON HERB SAUCE

SPRING VEGETABLE MEDLEY

CREAMY ASPARAGUS SOUP

TROPICAL COCONUT CAKE
WITH CREAMY COCONUT
FROSTING

Spinach and Mushroom Stuffed Pork Loin

Makes 10 to 12 servings

¼ cup butter
1 cup chopped onion
1 (8-ounce) package baby bella mushrooms
½ cup chopped red bell pepper
2 teaspoons minced garlic
1 (10-ounce) package frozen chopped spinach, squeezed dry
1 teaspoon chopped fresh rosemary
1 teaspoon salt, divided
½ teaspoon ground black pepper, divided
1 (5-ounce) package shredded Parmesan cheese
1 (5-pound) pork loin roast, trimmed
2 tablespoons olive oil
Lemon Herb Sauce (recipe follows)
Garnish: fresh rosemary

1. In a Dutch oven, heat butter over medium heat until melted. Add onion, mushrooms, red bell pepper, and garlic; cook for 10 minutes, stirring frequently, until tender. Add spinach, rosemary, ½ teaspoon salt, and ¼ teaspoon pepper, stirring to combine; cook for 3 minutes. Add cheese, stirring just until combined; set aside.

2. Preheat oven to 475°.

3. Place pork loin on a clean surface, and cut into one side of meat, leaving a ½-inch border. Continue cutting loin until it can be rolled out into a rectangle and is about ½ inch thick. Place a piece of heavy-duty plastic wrap on top of loin. Using a meat mallet, pound meat until it reaches an even thickness of about ½ inch. Spread spinach-mushroom filling evenly onto prepared loin, leaving a 1-inch border. Roll up lengthwise, jelly-roll fashion. Secure with butcher's twine. Rub outside of stuffed pork loin with olive oil, remaining ½ teaspoon salt, and remaining ¼ teaspoon pepper.

4. Place, seam side down, in a roasting pan. Bake for 20 minutes. Reduce heat to 325°; loosely cover with aluminum foil. Bake for 45 to 55 minutes or until a meat thermometer inserted into center of loin reaches 155°, or desired degree of doneness. Let stand for 10 minutes before slicing. Serve with Lemon Herb Sauce. Garnish with fresh rosemary, if desired.

Tip: Make roasted potatoes and a Spring Vegetable medley to accompany the pork.

Lemon Herb Sauce

Makes about 2 cups

¼ cup olive oil
2 tablespoons chopped fresh rosemary
2 tablespoons chopped fresh thyme
1 tablespoon dried oregano
1 tablespoon garlic powder
1 tablespoon all-purpose flour
2 cups chicken broth
1 tablespoon fresh lemon juice
½ teaspoon salt
½ teaspoon ground black pepper

1. In a small saucepan, heat olive oil over medium heat. Add rosemary, thyme, oregano, and garlic powder; cook for 3 minutes. Add flour; cook, stirring constantly, for 2 minutes. Gradually add chicken broth, whisking until smooth. Add lemon juice, salt, and pepper. Bring to a simmer; cook for 20 minutes, stirring occasionally, until sauce is slightly thickened.

Spring Vegetable Medley
Makes 8 to 10 servings

3   quarts water
1   tablespoon salt
1   pound baby carrots, trimmed and halved
    lengthwise
1   pound baby starburst squash
1   pound baby pattypan squash
¼   cup butter
2   tablespoons olive oil
1   (8-ounce) bag sugar snap peas
2   shallots, sliced
2   tablespoons minced garlic
1   tablespoon chopped fresh parsley
1   tablespoon chopped fresh chives
1   tablespoon fresh lemon juice
½   teaspoon salt
½   teaspoon ground black pepper

1. In a large Dutch oven, combine water and salt. Bring to a boil over high heat. Add carrots, return to a boil, and cook for 2 minutes. Add squash; cook for 3 to 4 minutes or until vegetables are crisp-tender. Remove vegetables from water; drain completely.
2. In Dutch oven, heat butter and olive oil over medium heat until butter is melted. Add sugar snap peas, shallots, and garlic; cook for 3 minutes, stirring frequently. Add carrots and squash; cook for 5 minutes, stirring frequently, until tender. Add parsley, chives, lemon juice, salt, and pepper; cook for 1 minute, stirring constantly.

Creamy Asparagus Soup
Makes 8 to 10 servings

¼   cup butter
2   tablespoons olive oil
2   pounds fresh asparagus, trimmed and chopped
2   cups chopped onion
2   cups chopped celery
1   tablespoon minced garlic
½   cup Riesling wine
⅓   cup all-purpose flour
6   cups chicken broth
1   cup heavy whipping cream
2   teaspoons sugar
1   teaspoon ground black pepper
½   teaspoon garlic powder
½   teaspoon salt
¼   teaspoon lemon zest
1   (8-ounce) package Monterey Jack cheese, grated
1½ cups finely grated Parmigiano-Reggiano cheese

1. In a Dutch oven, heat butter and olive oil over medium heat until butter is melted. Add asparagus, onion, celery, and garlic; cook for 8 minutes, stirring frequently. Add wine; cook for 2 minutes. Add flour; cook, stirring constantly, for 2 minutes. Gradually add chicken broth, whisking until smooth. Bring to a simmer, reduce heat to medium-low, and cook for 20 minutes, stirring occasionally. Remove from heat, and cool slightly.
2. In the container of a blender, purée asparagus mixture, in batches, until smooth. Return asparagus mixure to Dutch oven over medium heat. Add cream, sugar, pepper, garlic powder, salt, and lemon zest, whisking until smooth. Cook for 5 minutes or until soup is heated through. Add cheeses, stirring until cheeses are melted.

"For I remember it is Easter morn, And life and love and peace are all new born."

—Alice Freeman Palmer

Tropical Coconut Cake
Makes 1 (9-inch) cake

1½ cups unsalted butter, softened
2⅓ cups sugar, divided
6   large eggs, separated
3¾ cups cake flour
1½ teaspoons baking powder
½   teaspoon salt
1½ cups milk
1   teaspoon vanilla extract
1   teaspoon coconut extract
Pineapple Curd (recipe follows)
Creamy Coconut Frosting (recipe follows)
Garnish: toasted coconut, white chocolate curls

1. Preheat oven to 350°. Grease and flour 3 (9-inch) cake pans; set aside.
2. In a large bowl, combine butter and 2 cups sugar. Beat at high speed with an electric mixer until fluffy. Add egg yolks, one at a time, beating well after each addition. Sift together cake flour, baking powder, and salt. Add flour mixture to butter mixture alternately with milk, beginning and ending with flour mixture. Beat in vanilla and coconut extract.
3. In a separate bowl, beat egg whites at high speed with an electric mixer until soft peaks form. Add remaining ⅓ cup sugar, 1 tablespoon at a time, beating until stiff peaks form. Fold egg-white mixture into batter in thirds. Spoon batter into prepared pans. Bake for 25 to 27 minutes or until a wooden pick inserted in center comes out clean. Let cool in pans for 10 minutes.
4. Remove cake layers from pans, and cool completely on wire racks. Spread Pineapple Curd evenly between cake layers. Spread Creamy Coconut Frosting on sides and top of cake. Garnish sides of cake with toasted coconut. Top cake with white chocolate curls, if desired.

Pineapple Curd
Makes about 1¾ cups

¾   cup sugar
3   tablespoons cornstarch
2   (8-ounce) cans crushed pineapple, well drained
1   tablespoon fresh lemon juice
3   egg yolks, lightly beaten
¼   cup butter, cut into pieces
½   teaspoon pineapple extract

1. In a heavy saucepan, combine sugar and cornstarch. Add pineapple, lemon juice, and egg yolks. Cook over medium heat, stirring constantly, for 7 to 8 minutes or until very thick. Remove from heat; gradually whisk in

butter until melted. Stir in pineapple extract. Cool mixture slightly; cover and chill for 2 hours.

Creamy Coconut Frosting
Makes about 4 cups

2   (4-ounce) bars white baking chocolate, chopped*
¼   cup heavy whipping cream
½   cup butter, softened
½   cup sour cream
1   tablespoon coconut extract
5   cups confectioners' sugar

1. In a small bowl, combine white chocolate and cream. Microwave on High, in 30-second intervals, stirring between each, until melted and smooth (about 1½ minutes total). Set aside to cool completely.
2. In a large bowl, combine white chocolate mixture, butter, sour cream, and coconut extract. Beat at medium speed with an electric mixer until light and fluffy. Gradually add confectioners' sugar, beating until combined.

*We used Ghirardelli white chocolate premium baking bars. You may also substitute pineapple rum in place of pineapple extract, if preferred.

Tip: Toasted coconut lends an especially delicious taste and lots of texture to our tropical-themed cake. To toast coconut for garnish, place shredded coconut in a thin layer on a baking sheet, and bake at 350° until it is light brown, stirring every 30 seconds or so for a total of 3 to 4 minutes.

Whimsical Easter Elegance

Pick a couple of colors from a delicate floral china pattern to highlight on the table—we used vibrant pink and spring green. Classic crystal glassware and elegant flatware integrate seamlessly into the tablescape, and colorful Easter eggs at each setting add a playful touch to a cheerful spring table.

A Mother's
LOVE

·

Mom can hug away hurt and handle even the most difficult dilemmas.
When Mother's Day comes around, treat her to a day of pampering, starting
with a lovely breakfast in bed. Thoughtful details and sentimental gifts are sure
to convey your appreciation for all the ways she makes the world better.

MENU

SHIRRED EGGS BENEDICT
WITH LEMON-THYME
BUTTER SAUCE

MORNING PUNCH

Shirred Eggs Benedict with Lemon-Thyme Butter Sauce
Makes 6 servings

½   cup whole-wheat flour
½   cup all-purpose flour
1   tablespoon firmly packed light brown sugar
1   tablespoon chopped fresh thyme
1½ teaspoons baking powder
½   teaspoon salt
1   cup whole milk
1   large egg
¼   cup unsalted butter, melted
1   teaspoon butter extract
Shirred Eggs (recipe follows)
Lemon-Thyme Butter Sauce (recipe follows)
Garnish: fresh thyme sprigs, cherry tomatoes, pancetta
      cooked and chopped

1. In a medium bowl, combine whole-wheat flour, all-purpose flour, brown sugar, thyme, baking powder, and salt.
2. In a separate bowl, whisk together milk, egg, melted butter, and butter extract until well combined. Add milk mixture to flour mixture, whisking until smooth. Spoon about ¼ cup mixture into each waffle compartment of a waffle iron. Close cover, and cook for 2 to 4 minutes, or until done. Using a 3½-inch round cutter, cut waffles into rounds.
3. Place 1 waffle round on top of each Shirred Egg in muffin pan. Place a cutting board on top of pan. Carefully invert pan. Serve with Lemon-Thyme Butter Sauce. Garnish with fresh thyme, cherry tomatoes, and pancetta, if desired.

Shirred Eggs
Makes 6 servings

6   slices pancetta, cut into 6 (3-inch) rounds
6   large eggs
6   teaspoons Marsala
6   teaspoons half-and-half
2   tablespoons unsalted butter, softened
1   teaspoon salt
1   teaspoon ground black pepper

1. Preheat oven to 350°. Generously grease 6 jumbo muffin cups.
2. Place 1 pancetta round in bottom of each muffin cup. Crack 1 egg over each pancetta round. Spoon 1 teaspoon Marsala, 1 teaspoon half-and-half, and 1 teaspoon butter over each egg. Sprinkle evenly with salt and pepper. Bake 10 to 15 minutes, or to desired degree of doneness. Let cool in pan for 5 minutes.

Lemon-Thyme Butter Sauce
Makes about ½ cup

¼   cup Champagne vinegar
¼   cup vermouth
1   tablespoon minced shallots
1   tablespoon chopped fresh thyme
½   teaspoon salt
¼   teaspoon ground black pepper
2   large egg yolks
¼   cup unsalted butter, softened
3   tablespoons fresh lemon juice

1. In a small saucepan, combine vinegar, vermouth, shallots, thyme, salt, and pepper over medium-high heat. Bring to a boil, and cook for 5 to 6 minutes, stirring occasionally, until mixture is reduced to 2 tablespoons. Let cool for 5 minutes. Add egg yolks, whisking until smooth.
2. Transfer mixture to top of a double boiler over simmering water. Cook for 1 to 2 minutes, whisking constantly, until mixture begins to thicken. Remove from heat, and gradually whisk in butter until melted. Whisk in lemon juice. Serve immediately.

Morning Punch
Makes about ½ cup

3   (11.3-ounce) cans strawberry-banana nectar
1   (46-ounce) can pineapple juice
1   cup strawberry syrup
Garnish: fresh strawberries

1. In a large pitcher, combine strawberry-banana nectar, pineapple juice, and strawberry syrup. Garnish with fresh strawberries, if desired.

*"When you are a mother,
you are never really alone
in your thoughts. A
mother always has to think
twice, once for herself
and once for her child."*

—Sophia Loren

Teatime
SOCIAL

·

The flowers are in bloom, and the sun's warm rays are shining brightly in the sky. Take time to enjoy the fresh new day with an afternoon tea with a few friends to discuss an interesting book or to catch up on their lives. Spring is here!

MENU

DRIED APRICOT SCONES

HONEY-PISTACHIO CREAM

RADISH CUCUMBER TEA
SANDWICHES

CHOCOLATE MACAROONS
WITH STRAWBERRY FILLING

Dried Apricot Scones

Makes 8 scones

2½ cups all-purpose flour
½   cup plus 2 teaspoons sugar, divided
2   teaspoons baking powder
½   teaspoon salt
½   cup cold butter, cut into pieces
1   cup finely chopped dried apricots
1   cup plus 1 tablespoon heavy whipping cream,
    divided

1. Preheat oven to 375°. Line a baking sheet with parchment paper.
2. In a large bowl, combine flour, ½ cup sugar, baking powder, and salt. Using a pastry blender, cut butter into flour mixture until crumbly. Add apricots, stirring to mix well. Add 1 cup cream, stirring just until dry ingredients are moistened.
3. On a lightly floured surface, pat dough into an 8x½-inch circle. Cut scones into 8 equal wedges. Place on prepared baking sheet. Brush tops of scones with remaining 1 tablespoon cream, and sprinkle with remaining 2 teaspoons sugar. Bake for 20 minutes or until lightly browned.

Honey-Pistachio Cream

Makes 1¼ cups

1   (3-ounce) package cream cheese, softened
¼   cup sour cream
2   tablespoons honey
½   cup heavy whipping cream
½   cup very finely chopped roasted, salted pistachios

1. In a medium bowl, combine cream cheese, sour cream, and honey. Beat at medium speed with an electric mixer until smooth. Add cream; beat until stiff peaks form. Cover and chill. Immediately before serving, stir in pistachios.

Tip: Honey-Pistachio Cream can be made two or three days ahead of time. Keep refrigerated, adding pistachios just before serving.

Radish Cucumber Tea Sandwiches

Makes 1 dozen

¼   cup butter, softened
2   teaspoons minced chives
6   very thin slices white sandwich bread*, crusts
    removed
1   medium seedless cucumber, thinly sliced
8 to 10 medium radishes, thinly sliced
Coarse kosher salt
Garnish: crème fraîche, mizuna mustard microgreens,
    minced chives

1. In a small bowl, combine butter and chives; set aside.
2. Cut bread slices in half lengthwise. Spread a thin layer of butter mixture on each bread slice. Alternately layer sliced cucumber and sliced radishes on top of butter mixture. Sprinkle with kosher salt to taste. Garnish with crème fraîche, microgreens, and minced chives, if desired.

*We used Pepperidge Farm Very Thin Sliced White Sandwich Bread.

Tip: Crème fraîche and microgreens are available at gourmet and specialty markets. Broccoli sprouts or alfalfa sprouts may be substituted for the microgreens, and sour cream may be substituted for the crème fraîche.

Chocolate Macaroons with Strawberry Filling
Makes about 2 dozen

¾ cup slivered almonds, toasted
2 cups confectioners' sugar*
2 tablespoons unsweetened Dutch-processed cocoa powder
3 egg whites, room temperature
½ teaspoon vanilla extract
2 tablespoons sugar
Strawberry Filling (recipe follows)

1. Preheat oven to 275°. Line baking sheets with parchment paper or silicone baking mats; set aside.
2. In the work bowl of a food processor, pulse almonds until very finely ground. Add confectioners' sugar and cocoa; process until well combined.
3. In a medium bowl, combine egg whites and vanilla. Beat at high speed with an electric mixer until frothy. Gradually add sugar, beating until stiff peaks form. Fold almond mixture into egg-white mixture until well combined. Let batter stand for 15 minutes.
4. Spoon batter into a large pastry bag fitted with a round tip. Pipe batter in 1½-inch rounds, 2 inches apart, onto prepared baking sheets. Let cookies stand at room temperature for 45 minutes before baking. (This helps develop the signature crisp exterior.) Bake for 16 to 18 minutes or until firm to the touch. Let cool on pans completely.
5. Spread Strawberry Filling in the center of the flat side of 1 cookie, and sandwich 2 cookies together. Repeat with remaining filling and cookies. Store cookies in an airtight container.

Strawberry Filling
Makes about ¾ cup

2 (3-ounce) packages cream cheese, softened
½ cup butter, softened
½ cup strawberry preserves
¼ cup confectioners' sugar

1. In a small bowl, combine cream cheese, butter, preserves, and confectioners' sugar. Beat at medium speed with an electric mixer until creamy.

Tip: Proper measuring is the secret to successful baking. Firmly packed ingredients will give you varying and often disappointing results, so when measuring dry ingredients be sure to use the following measuring method: Fluff up the flour, and sprinkle into a dry measuring cup. Scrape off the excess flour with a straight edge.

"A friend knows the song in my heart and sings it to me when my memory fails."
—Donna Roberts

Tea for Two

Fluff up your porch with pillows, throws, and other comfortable linen accents for this casual and intimate gathering. Supplement live potted plants with a few cut blooms in small vases, and bring a little indoor elegance outside with fine floral china and silver flatware pieces.

Just
DESSERTS

Strawberry Charlotte
Makes 1 (8½-inch) charlotte

2 (3-ounce) packages ladyfingers, split
¼ cup cold water
1 (0.25-ounce) envelope unflavored gelatin
1 (8-ounce) package cream cheese, softened
¼ cup unsalted butter, softened
¼ cup strawberry syrup
2 teaspoons strawberry extract
1 cup confectioners' sugar
2 cups heavy whipping cream
1 tablespoon sugar
1 (1-pound) container fresh strawberries, divided
¼ cup strawberry jelly, melted

1. Line bottom of an 8½-inch spring-form pan with waxed paper. Lightly spray the bottom and sides with cooking spray. Line the bottom and sides of the pan with ladyfingers, making sure they fit together snugly.
2. In a small microwave-safe bowl, combine cold water and gelatin; let stand 5 minutes. Microwave on High until dissolved (approximately 15 seconds total); cool slightly.
3. In a medium bowl, combine cream cheese, butter, strawberry syrup, and strawberry extract. Beat at medium speed with an electric mixer until creamy. Gradually add confectioners' sugar, mixing well; set aside.
4. In a separate bowl, beat cream and sugar at high speed until soft peaks form. Beat in dissolved gelatin until stiff peaks form. Gently combine cream cheese mixture and whipped cream mixture.

5. To assemble, evenly spread half of cream mixture over ladyfingers in bottom of pan. Place an even layer of sliced strawberries on top of cream mixture. Spoon remaining half of cream mixture over strawberries. Cover with plastic wrap, and chill for at least 4 hours.
6. To serve, remove plastic wrap, and carefully run a knife around the edge of the springform pan. Carefully un-latch ring of springform pan, and un-mold. Arrange remaining sliced strawberries on top of cream mixture. Brush strawberries with melted strawberry jelly.

Lemon Cheesecake Squares
Makes 2 dozen

2¼ cups all-purpose flour, divided
½ cup confectioners' sugar
1 cup butter, softened
½ cup finely chopped unsalted cashews
2 (8-ounce) packages cream cheese, softened
2¼ cups sugar, divided
½ cup milk
1 teaspoon lemon extract
4 large eggs
2 teaspoons lemon zest
⅓ cup fresh lemon juice
½ teaspoon baking powder
Garnish: confectioners' sugar, fresh raspberries, lemon zest

1. Preheat oven to 350°.
2. In a medium bowl, combine 2 cups flour and confectioners' sugar. Using a pastry blender, cut in butter until mixture is crumbly; stir in cashews.

Press mixture evenly into bottom of a 13x9-inch baking pan; bake for 15 minutes.
3. In a medium bowl, combine cream cheese and ½ cup sugar; beat at medium speed with an electric mixer until smooth. Add milk and lemon extract, beating until well combined; pour over crust. Bake for 15 minutes; remove from oven, and cool for 10 minutes.
4. In a medium bowl, whisk together remaining 1¾ cups sugar, eggs, lemon zest, and lemon juice.
5. In a small bowl, combine remaining ¼ cup flour and baking powder; add to sugar mixture, whisking to com-bine. Pour sugar mixture over cream cheese mixture. Bake for 40 minutes, or until a wooden pick inserted in cen-ter comes out slightly sticky. Cut into squares, and garnish with confection-ers' sugar, raspberries, and lemon zest, if desired.

Summer

*Fireworks, picnics, and lakeside excursions—the celebrations
heat up as all ages bask in the sunny glow of summer. Gather
the family, and enjoy Southern-style entertaining.*

Time for DAD

He has picked us up when we've fallen. He is always there to lend an ear,
a hand, or encouragement. He has beamed with pride to call us his own.
Father's Day is an occasion to envelop Dad in love and thank him
for his guidance that help mold us into better people.

MENU

SUMMER GARDEN SALAD
WITH BALSAMIC VINAIGRETTE

OVERSTUFFED TWICE-
BAKED POTATOES

SPICY MARINATED FILETS

VANILLA BEAN ICE CREAM
WITH BLUEBERRY WINE SAUCE

Summer Garden Salad with Balsamic Vinaigrette
Makes 4 servings

8   cups mixed salad greens
1   cup halved grape tomatoes
1   cup thinly sliced seedless cucumber
1   yellow bell pepper, sliced into ¼-inch strips
¾   cup thinly sliced radishes
½   cup thinly sliced red onion
Balsamic Vinaigrette (recipe follows)

1. In a large bowl, combine salad greens, tomatoes, cucumber, bell pepper, radishes, and onion. Drizzle with dressing just before serving.

Balsamic Vinaigrette
Makes about 1⅓ cups

½   cup balsamic vinegar
2   tablespoons dark brown sugar
2   tablespoons stone-ground mustard
½   teaspoon garlic salt
¼   teaspoon ground black pepper
½   cup light olive oil

1. In a small bowl, combine vinegar, brown sugar, mustard, garlic salt, and pepper. Whisk until sugar is dissolved. Slowly whisk in oil. Cover and refrigerate until ready to serve. Whisk before serving. Store in the refrigerator in an airtight container for up to 2 weeks.

until cream cheese and butter are melted. Add bacon, sour cream, 1 cup cheese, green onion, salt, and pepper; stir to combine well. Spoon potato mixture into shells.
4. Return filled shells to prepared baking sheet. Return potatoes to oven, and bake for 20 to 25 minutes or until lightly browned and bubbly. Remove from oven, and top with remaining ½ cup cheese. Serve immediately. Garnish with crumbled bacon and green onion, if desired.

Spicy Marinated Filets
Makes 4 servings

1   cup water
¾   cup low-sodium soy sauce
½   cup red-wine vinegar
3   tablespoons Worcestershire sauce
2   tablespoons minced garlic
1   tablespoon fresh lemon juice
1   tablespoon dried basil
2   teaspoons ground black pepper
1   teaspoon ground red pepper
½   teaspoon onion powder
¼   cup olive oil
4   (8-ounce) beef tenderloin steaks

1. In a medium bowl, combine water, soy sauce, vinegar, Worcestershire sauce, garlic, lemon juice, basil, black pepper, red pepper, and onion powder. Slowly drizzle in olive oil, whisking to combine well. Place steaks in a large resealable plastic bag; pour marinade over steaks. Seal bag, and chill for at least 4 to 6 hours, turning occasionally.
2. Remove steaks from marinade; set marinade aside. Grill steaks, covered with grill lid, over medium-high heat, (350° to 400°) for 8 to 10 minutes on each side or to desired degree of doneness.
3. In a small saucepan, bring reserved marinade to a medium boil, and heat for 5 minutes.

Overstuffed Twice-Baked Potatoes
Makes 4 servings

4   large baking potatoes, washed and dried
Olive oil
8   pieces thick-sliced bacon
1   large yellow onion, thinly sliced
1   (3-ounce) package cream cheese, softened
½   cup butter, cut into pieces
½   cup sour cream
1½   cups grated white Cheddar cheese, divided
2   tablespoons chopped green onion
½   teaspoon salt
¼   teaspoon ground black pepper
Garnish: crumbled bacon, green onion

1. Preheat oven to 350°. Line a baking sheet with aluminum foil. Rub potatoes with olive oil to coat skins. Place on prepared baking sheet. Bake for 55 to 65 minutes or until potatoes are fork-tender. Cool until easy to handle.
2. In a large skillet, cook bacon over medium heat for 15 minutes or until browned and crispy. Remove bacon, and crumble; set aside. Reserve 3 tablespoons bacon drippings in skillet. Add onion; cook, covered, over medium-high heat for 20 minutes, stirring occasionally. Cut a thin slice off top of each potato lengthwise, being careful not to damage skins. Using a melon baller or spoon, scoop out pulp, leaving ¼-inch-thick shells.
3. In a medium bowl, combine potato pulp, cream cheese, and butter. Using a potato masher, mash potato mixture

Vanilla Bean Ice Cream
Makes 1 gallon

9   cups milk, divided
1   (12-ounce) can evaporated milk
1   cup sugar
2   vanilla beans, split lengthwise and scraped
3   large eggs, lightly beaten
1   (14-ounce) can sweetened condensed milk
1   (3.4-ounce) package instant vanilla pudding mix
1   tablespoon fresh lemon juice
1½ teaspoons vanilla extract
Blueberry Wine Sauce (recipe follows)
Garnish: fresh mint

1. In a medium saucepan, combine 4 cups milk, evaporated milk, sugar, and vanilla bean seeds over medium heat. Cook for 8 to 10 minutes, stirring occasionally, until milk is heated and sugar is dissolved; do not boil. Gradually add 2 cups hot milk mixture to eggs, beating to combine well. Pour egg mixture into remaining hot milk mixture, whisking constantly. Cook for 2 minutes, whisking constantly. Remove from heat; let cool for 30 minutes.
2. In a large bowl, combine milk mixture, condensed milk, pudding mix, lemon juice, and vanilla, whisking to combine well. Cover and chill completely. Add remaining 5 cups milk, stirring to combine well. Pour ice-cream mixture into container of an ice-cream freezer, and freeze according to manufacturer's instructions.
3. Spoon ice cream into a freezer-safe container, and freeze for at least 4 hours for a firmer texture. Serve with Blueberry Wine Sauce. Garnish with fresh mint, if desired.

Blueberry Wine Sauce
Makes about 2½ cups

1   cup sugar
1   cup water
2   tablespoons fresh lemon juice
2   cups blueberry wine
2   cups fresh blueberries

1. In a medium saucepan, combine sugar, water, and lemon juice. Bring to a simmer, stirring frequently, until sugar dissolves. Add wine; cook until mixture reaches 225° on a candy thermometer, stirring frequently. Remove from heat; add blueberries, stirring to combine well. Serve warm or at room temperature. Store, covered, in refrigerator.

"Everything I ever learned as a small boy came from my father. And I never found anything he ever told me to be wrong or worthless. The simple lessons he taught me are as sharp and clear in my mind, as if I had heard them only yesterday."

—Philip Dunne

Dad's Day

Golf ball place cards on a green place mat give a little tongue-in-cheek flavor to this fatherly celebration. Lean on more masculine colors like blues, reds, and greens paired with natural accents to pull together the overall look.

MENU

**COCONUT SHRIMP WITH
CARIBBEAN DIPPING SAUCE**

**KEY LIME
CHEESECAKE SQUARES**

AIMEE'S BLUE WAVE

Summer *Fun on the*
FOURTH

Fireworks, fireflies, and friends. Blast off Fourth of July festivities with a lovely outdoor celebration that includes good food and water views. For many, this is the time for an escape to the beach or the lake with friends and loved ones. Make this holiday even more special with a summery seafood menu.

Coconut Shrimp with Caribbean Dipping Sauce
Makes about 3 dozen (12 servings)

Vegetable oil for frying
1   cup all-purpose flour
1   tablespoon Caribbean jerk seasoning
2   large eggs
2   tablespoons water
1¼ cups panko (Japanese bread crumbs)
1¼ cups unsweetened flaked coconut
2   pounds peeled and deveined fresh large shrimp,
     tails left on
Caribbean Dipping Sauce (recipe follows)
Garnish: Caribbean jerk seasoning

1. In a Dutch oven, pour oil to a depth of 2 inches; heat to 350°. Line a baking sheet with parchment paper. Set aside.
2. In a shallow dish, combine flour and Caribbean jerk seasoning. In a separate shallow dish, combine eggs and water; beat with fork until well combined.
3. In another shallow dish, combine bread crumbs and coconut. Coat shrimp with flour, shaking off excess. Dip floured shrimp into egg mixture, allowing excess to drain. Coat shrimp in bread crumb mixture. Place on prepared baking sheet. Fry shrimp, in batches, for 1 to 2 minutes or until golden brown. Drain on paper towels. Serve with Caribbean Dipping Sauce, and sprinkle with additional Caribbean jerk seasoning, if desired.

Caribbean Dipping Sauce
Makes 1½ cups

1   tablespoon butter
2   teaspoons minced garlic
2   teaspoons grated ginger
1   habañero pepper, seeded and minced
1   (18-ounce) jar orange marmalade
3   tablespoons fresh lime juice
1   tablespoon whole-grain mustard
1   teaspoon prepared horseradish
½   teaspoon salt

1. In a medium saucepan, melt butter over medium-high heat. Add garlic, ginger, and habañero pepper; cook for 2 minutes, stirring constantly. Reduce heat to medium-low. Add marmalade, lime juice, mustard, horseradish, and salt. Simmer for 5 minutes, stirring frequently. Serve warm.

Key Lime Cheesecake Squares
Makes 2 dozen

2   cups graham-cracker crumbs
1   cup finely chopped macadamia nuts
2¾   cups sugar, divided
6   tablespoons butter, melted
1   egg white, lightly beaten
2   (8-ounce) packages cream cheese, softened
½   cup evaporated milk
4   large eggs
2   tablespoons Key lime zest
⅓   cup fresh Key lime juice
¼   cup all-purpose flour
½   teaspoon baking powder
Garnish: confectioners' sugar, Key lime slices

1. Preheat oven to 350°.
2. In a medium bowl, combine graham-cracker crumbs, macadamia nuts, ½ cup sugar, and melted butter. Add beaten egg white, stirring to combine well. Press mixture evenly into bottom of a 13x9-inch baking pan; bake for 8 minutes.
3. In a medium bowl, combine cream cheese and ½ cup sugar; beat at medium speed with an electric mixer until smooth. Add evaporated milk, beating until well combined. Spoon cream cheese mixture evenly over crust. Bake for 15 minutes; remove from oven, and let cool for 10 minutes.
4. In a medium bowl, combine remaining 1¾ cups sugar, eggs, lime zest, and lime juice, whisking to combine well.
5. In a small bowl, combine flour and baking powder; add to sugar mixture, whisking to combine. Pour sugar

mixture over cream cheese mixture. Bake for 40 minutes, or until a wooden pick inserted in center comes out slightly sticky. Let cool completely. Cut into squares. Garnish with confectioners' sugar and Key lime slices, if desired.

Aimee's Blue Wave
Makes 1 drink

1½   ounces lime-flavored vodka
1   ounce blue curaçao
1   ounce fresh lime juice
Simple Syrup (recipe follows)
Garnish: kiwifruit slices

1. Fill a cocktail shaker halfway with ice cubes. Add lime-flavored vodka, blue curaçao, lime juice, and Simple Syrup to shaker. Shake mixture vigorously for 5 to 10 seconds. Strain mixture into chilled cocktail glass. Garnish with kiwifruit slices, if desired.

Simple Syrup
Makes about 1½ cups

1   cup sugar
1   cup water

1. In a small saucepan, combine sugar and water over medium-high heat, stirring constantly. Bring mixture to a boil; reduce heat to low, and simmer for 3 to 4 minutes, stirring constantly. Remove from heat, and cool completely. Pour into an airtight container. Store syrup in refrigerator for up to 3 weeks.

Ladies Dessert
TEA

·

When summer sizzles outside, have your friends break out their favorite sundresses and bring the party inside with a playful and girly tea. Plentiful sweets on an assortment of floral china and crisp linens make up the party-ready details.

MENU

LOREN'S PINK PARASOLS

CHIM CHIM CHERRY SCONES

SPOONFUL OF SUGAR
TEACAKES WITH
CREAM CHEESE ICING

RASPBERRY ICE

5. Bake for 10 to 12 minutes or until lightly browned. Cool on pans for 2 minutes. Remove to wire racks, and cool completely. Paint cookies with Colored Icing. Decorate with dragées and sanding sugar, if desired.

Colored Icing
Makes 2½ cups

¼ cup water
3 tablespoons meringue powder
2 cups confectioners' sugar, sifted
Pink gel paste food coloring

1. In a small bowl, whisk together water and meringue powder until frothy. Add confectioners' sugar, whisking until smooth.
2. Divide mixture into 2 separate bowls. In 1 bowl, whisk in food coloring until desired color is reached. Use immediately; cover tightly with plastic wrap when not in use.

Chim Chim Cherry Scones
Makes 1 dozen

3 cups all-purpose flour
6 tablespoons sugar
½ teaspoon baking powder
½ teaspoon baking soda
½ teaspoon salt
½ cup cold butter, cut into pieces
½ cup finely chopped maraschino cherries
1 cup plus 1 tablespoon heavy whipping
   cream, divided
½ cup sour cream
3 tablespoons maraschino cherry juice

1. Preheat oven to 450°. Line a baking sheet with parchment paper.
2. In a large bowl, combine flour, sugar, baking powder, baking soda, and salt. Using a pastry blender, cut butter into flour mixture until crumbly. Stir in chopped cherries.
3. In a small bowl, combine 1 cup cream, sour cream, and cherry juice, whisking until smooth. Add cream mixture to flour mixture, stirring just until dry ingredients are moistened (dough will be sticky).
4. On a lightly floured surface, with floured hands, press dough to 1-inch thickness. Using a 2-inch square cutter, cut out scones, and place on prepared baking sheet. Brush tops of scones with remaining 1 tablespoon cream. Bake for 15 to 17 minutes or until lightly browned.

Loren's Pink Parasols
Makes about 2½ dozen

1½ cups unsalted butter, softened
1   cup confectioners' sugar
½   teaspoon vanilla extract
3   cups all-purpose flour
½   teaspoon salt
Colored Icing (recipe follows)
Garnishes: pink dragées, pink sanding sugar

1. In a medium bowl, beat butter and sugar at medium speed with an electric mixer until creamy. Beat in vanilla.
2. In a separate bowl, whisk together flour and salt. Gradually add flour mixture to butter mixture, beating at medium-low speed until well combined. Divide dough into thirds; wrap each portion of dough tightly in plastic wrap, and refrigerate for 2 hours.
3. Preheat oven to 375°. Line baking sheets with parchment paper; set aside.
4. On a lightly floured surface, roll each portion of dough to ¼-inch thickness. Using a 5-inch umbrella-shaped cookie cutter, cut out dough. Place cookies 1 inch apart on prepared pans.

Spoonful of Sugar Teacakes

Makes 2 dozen

1 cup butter, softened
2 cups sugar
4 large eggs
2 teaspoons vanilla extract
3 cups all-purpose flour
1 tablespoon baking powder
½ teaspoon salt
1 cup whole milk
½ cup sour cream
Cream Cheese Icing (recipe follows)
Garnish: Sugared Fruit, Mint, and Zest (recipe follows)

1. Preheat oven to 350°. Spray a 13x9-inch baking pan with nonstick baking spray with flour.
2. In a large bowl, beat butter and sugar at medium speed with an electric mixer until fluffy. Add eggs, one at a time, beating well after each addition. Beat in vanilla.
3. In a medium bowl, combine flour, baking powder, and salt. Gradually add flour mixture to butter mixture alternately with milk, beginning and ending with flour mixture. Beat until well combined. Beat in sour cream. Spread batter evenly into prepared pan.
4. Bake for 35 to 40 minutes or until a wooden pick inserted in center comes out clean. Cool in pan on a wire rack for 10 minutes. Remove from pan, and cool completely on wire rack.
5. Trim ½ inch off each side of cake. Level cake by using a serrated knife to trim off rounded top. Cut cake into 3x2-inch pieces. Spoon Cream Cheese Icing on top of each cake piece. Garnish with Sugared Fruit, Mint, and Zest, if desired.

Cream Cheese Icing

Makes about 2 cups

1 (8-ounce) package cream cheese, softened
2 cups confectioners' sugar
¼ cup whole milk

1. In a medium bowl, combine cream cheese and confectioners' sugar. Beat at medium-low speed with an electric mixer until smooth. Add milk, beating until smooth.

Sugared Fruit, Mint, and Zest

Makes about 2 cups

1 egg white
1 tablespoon water
Fresh raspberries
Fresh mint sprigs
Sugar
Lemon Zest
Orange Zest

1. In a small bowl, whisk together egg white and water. Using a small paintbrush, brush raspberries and mint with egg white mixture. Sprinkle with sugar, shaking off excess. Place on a baking sheet lined with parchment paper to dry. Toss lemon zest and orange zest in sugar to coat. Place on baking sheet to dry.

Raspberry Ice

Makes 12 servings

4 pints fresh raspberries
3 cups water
2¼ cups sugar
½ (1-ounce) package fresh mint
¼ cup fresh lemon juice
Garnish: fresh raspberries, fresh mint

1. In the work bowl of a food processor, process raspberries until puréed. Press purée through a fine-mesh strainer, discarding solids; set aside.
2. In a medium saucepan, combine water and sugar; cook over medium-high heat, stirring until sugar dissolves. Add mint. Bring mixture to a boil; reduce heat to low, and simmer for 3 to 4 minutes. Remove from heat, and cool completely. Remove and discard mint. Add raspberry purée and lemon juice to sugar mixture, stirring well.
3. Pour into a 13x9-inch baking pan, and place in freezer. Freeze for 4 hours or until no liquid remains, scraping frozen mixture every hour with a fork until fluffy. Garnish with raspberries and mint, if desired.

Just DESSERTS

Chocolate Peanut Butter Cake

Makes 1 (9-inch) cake

¾ cup butter, softened
2¼ cups sugar
1 cup creamy peanut butter
6 large eggs
3¾ cups sifted all-purpose flour
2½ teaspoons baking powder
1 teaspoon salt
1¼ cups milk
2 teaspoons vanilla extract
Chocolate Fudge Frosting
    (recipe follows)
Garnish: chopped honey-roasted
    peanuts

1. Preheat oven to 350°. Grease and flour 3 (9-inch) cake pans.
2. In a large bowl, beat butter and sugar at medium speed with an electric mixer until fluffy. Add peanut butter; beat until creamy. Add eggs, one at a time, beating well after each addition.
3. In a small bowl, combine flour, baking powder, and salt. Add flour mixture to butter mixture alternately with milk, beginning and ending with flour mixture. Beat in vanilla. Spoon batter into prepared pans. Bake for 25 to 27 minutes or until a wooden pick inserted in center comes out clean. Cool in pans for 10 minutes; remove to wire rack, and cool completely. Spread Chocolate Fudge Frosting between layers and on top and sides of cake. Garnish with peanuts, if desired.

Chocolate Fudge Frosting

Makes 4 cups

1 cup sugar
½ cup firmly packed dark brown sugar
1 cup heavy whipping cream
½ cup milk
8 (1-ounce) squares semisweet baking chocolate, chopped
4 tablespoons butter
1 cup confectioners' sugar

1. In a large saucepan, combine sugar, brown sugar, cream, milk, and chocolate over medium heat. Bring to a boil, stirring frequently with a wire whisk. Reduce heat to medium-low; simmer for 20 minutes or until thickened, stirring frequently.
2. Remove from heat. Whisk in butter, one tablespoon at a time, until butter is completely melted. Pour into a 13x9-inch pan. Refrigerate for 1½ hours.
3. Place chocolate mixture in a medium bowl. Beat at high speed with an electric mixer for 2 minutes or until light and fluffy. Gradually add confectioners' sugar, mixing well.

Jo's Whipping Cream Pound Cake

Makes 1 (9-inch) cake

1 cup butter, softened
3 cups sugar
5 large eggs
3 cups cake flour
1 (8-ounce) container whipping cream
1½ teaspoons vanilla extract

1. Preheat oven to 325°. Grease and flour tube cake pan.
2. In a large bowl, beat butter and sugar at medium speed with an electric mixer until fluffy. Add eggs, one at a time, beating well after each addition. Add flour to butter mixture alternately with cream, beginning and ending with flour. Add vanilla; beat for 4 minutes.
3. Pour batter into prepared pan. Bake for 1 hour and 15 minutes or until a wooden pick inserted into center comes out clean. Turn out onto plate, then turn over onto wire rack to cool.

Tip: For best results, butter and eggs should be at room temperature. Serve with a basic glaze, if desired. Also, you can easily alter this basic pound cake recipe and turn it into "cup" cakes as shown above. Simply pour the batter into miniature oven-safe baking cups, and monitor the baking time.

Fall

Dazzling fall colors are matched only by the warmth of gracious autumn gatherings. All of creation, resplendent in her orange, red, and gold finery, beckons the heart to gratitude. Step into the great outdoors, and enjoy an abundant harvest.

MENU

PULLED PORK

CHEESY CORNBREAD

FENNEL SLAW

OATMEAL-CHOCOLATE
CREAM PIES

Harvest FESTIVAL

Sizzling summer fades into blissful autumn as cooling temperatures and changing colors spark outdoor celebrations. Set the mood with a luscious fall-inspired tablescape, and fill your guests' plates with make-ahead dishes, ensuring that once the party starts, your time will be spent mingling with guests instead of over a grill.

4. Adjust oven rack to lower-middle position, and preheat oven to 325°. Line a roasting pan with aluminum foil; place a wire rack in pan.

5. Remove pork from brine, discarding brine; dry pork thoroughly with paper towels. Rub entire surface of pork with mustard mixture, and sprinkle with spice mixture. Place pork on prepared wire rack. Place a sheet of parchment paper over pork, then cover pan with aluminum foil, sealing edges to prevent moisture from escaping.

6. Bake for 4 hours. Remove from oven; discard foil and parchment paper. Carefully pour liquid in bottom of pan into a fat separator; reserve cooking liquid for sauce.

7. Return pork to oven, and cook, uncovered, for about 2 hours or until well browned and tender and a meat thermometer inserted into thickest portion of pork registers 200°. Transfer pork to a serving dish, and tent loosely with foil; let rest for 20 minutes. Using 2 forks, shred pork into bite-size pieces.

8. In a medium saucepan, combine ¾ cup reserved defatted cooking liquid, onion, and garlic. Bring to a simmer, and cook for 5 minutes or until onion is tender. Add ketchup, vinegar, Worcestershire sauce, and brown sugar. Bring to a boil, whisking occasionally. Serve with pork.

Pulled Pork
Makes 8 to 10 servings

1   cup plus 2 teaspoons kosher salt, divided
½   cup plus 2 tablespoons sugar, divided
3   tablespoons plus 2 teaspoons liquid smoke, divided
4   quarts cold water
1   (7-pound) boneless pork butt, cut in half horizontally
¼   cup whole-grain mustard
2   tablespoons ground black pepper
2   tablespoons smoked paprika
1   teaspoon ground red pepper
1½ cups finely minced yellow onion
2   teaspoons minced garlic
1⅓ cups ketchup
1   cup apple-cider vinegar
⅓   cup Worcestershire sauce
¼   cup firmly packed light brown sugar

1. In a 6-quart bowl, dissolve 1 cup salt, ½ cup sugar, and 3 tablespoons liquid smoke in 4 quarts cold water to make a brine. Submerge pork in brine, and cover with plastic wrap; refrigerate for at least 2 hours.

2. In a small bowl, combine mustard and remaining 2 teaspoons liquid smoke; set aside.

3. In a second small bowl, combine black pepper, paprika, red pepper, remaining 2 tablespoons sugar, and remaining 2 teaspoons salt; set aside.

Cheesy Cornbread
Makes 8 servings

1   (1-pound) package hardwood-smoked bacon
1   large Vidalia onion, chopped
2½ cups self-rising yellow cornmeal mix
1   cup all-purpose flour
1   cup shredded Cheddar cheese
½   cup sugar
1   (0.75-ounce) package fresh chives, chopped
1   teaspoon kosher salt
1   teaspoon ground black pepper
1½ cups whole buttermilk
3   large eggs, lightly beaten
2   tablespoons vegetable oil

1. Preheat oven to 350°.

2. In a 9-inch square cast-iron skillet, cook bacon over medium heat until crisp. Place bacon on paper towels to drain, and reserve bacon drippings in a heat-proof container.

3. Add onion to skillet, and cook over medium-high heat until onion begins to caramelize; remove from skillet, and set aside. Return reserved bacon drippings to skillet, and place in oven to heat.

4. In a large bowl, combine cornmeal mix, flour, cheese, sugar, chives, salt, and pepper. In a small bowl, whisk (Recipes continued on page 59)

Oatmeal-Chocolate Cream Pies
Recipe on page 59

together buttermilk and eggs; add to cornmeal mixture, whisking until well combined. Crumble bacon; stir bacon and cooked onion into batter. Pour into prepared skillet.

5. Bake for 30 to 35 minutes, or until golden and a wooden pick inserted in the center comes out clean. Let cool in pan for 10 minutes. Remove cornbread to a wire rack to cool completely. Cut cornbread in half crosswise, then cut vertically into quarters (8 slices total).

6. Brush grill rack with vegetable oil. Grill cornbread slices over medium heat (300° to 350°) for 3 to 4 minutes on each side or until heated through. Serve with Pulled Pork and sauce.

Fennel Slaw
Makes 8 to 10 servings

2 large carrots, thinly sliced
2 medium fennel bulbs, quartered and thinly sliced
2 bunches green onions, cut into ½-inch slices
1 green apple, halved, cored, and cut into thin strips
2 tablespoons finely chopped fennel fronds
¾ cup Champagne vinegar
½ cup extra-light olive oil
1½ teaspoons kosher salt
1½ teaspoons ground black pepper

1. In a large bowl, combine carrots, fennel, green onions, apple, fennel fronds, vinegar, olive oil, salt, and pepper. Cover and refrigerate for at least 6 hours or overnight.

Oatmeal-Chocolate Cream Pies
Makes 10 (4-inch) pies

1   cup all-purpose flour
¾   cup regular oats
½   cup firmly packed light brown sugar
¼   teaspoon kosher salt
10 tablespoons unsalted butter, chilled and cut into pieces
1   tablespoon heavy whipping cream
½   teaspoon vanilla extract
12 (1-ounce) squares semisweet chocolate, melted
1¾ cups sugar, divided
4   tablespoons water
2   tablespoons light corn syrup
6   egg whites, room temperature

1. In the work bowl of a food processor, combine flour, oats, sugar, and salt. Pulse until combined. Add butter; pulse until mixture resembles coarse crumbs. With processor running, add cream and vanilla; process until dough comes together. Wrap dough tightly in plastic wrap. Refrigerate for 2 hours or until firm.

2. On a lightly floured surface, roll dough to ⅛-inch thickness. Fit dough into 10 (4-inch) tart pans with removable bottoms, pressing into bottoms and up sides of pans. Freeze for 30 minutes or until very firm.

3. Preheat oven to 350°. Prick bottom and sides of dough with a fork. Bake for 15 to 18 minutes or until edges are golden brown. Transfer tart shells to a wire rack to cool.

4. Pour melted chocolate evenly into bottoms of prepared tart shells. Let stand until chocolate sets.

5. Meanwhile, in a small heavy-bottomed saucepan, combine 1½ cups sugar, water, and corn syrup. Heat over medium heat, stirring occasionally, until sugar dissolves. (Once sugar dissolves, do not stir anymore.) Bring mixture to a boil. Cook until a candy thermometer registers 230°, 6 to 10 minutes, brushing sides of pan occasionally with a pastry brush dipped in cold water to prevent sugar from crystallizing. Remove from heat.

6. Beat egg whites at medium speed with an electric mixer until soft peaks form. Gradually add remaining ¼ cup sugar. Reduce speed to medium-low, and pour hot sugar mixture in a thin, steady stream down side of bowl into egg white mixture. Increase mixer speed to medium, and beat until cool, about 5 to 10 minutes. (Frosting should be thick and shiny.) Immediately spoon frosting into each prepared tart. Let stand for 5 minutes before serving.

Autumn Elegance

Set the tone for your table with a profusion of seasonal blooms. Patterned runners in coordinating colors can be easily made with a favorite fabric. Sturdy pewter cups and chargers add weight to the look of classic white dinnerware. Pair indoor chairs with rustic tables and benches to expand your outdoor seating.

Hearty Fall
POTLUCK

·

*Pumpkin-hued leaves and fall flowers decorate the natural landscape as
cooler temperatures call for warm and familiar comfort foods. Invite your
friends to share their family's favorite variation on classic soups and stews
for a potluck evening filled with good food and fond remembrances.*

MENU

**CHICKEN AND
ANDOUILLE GUMBO**

GARLIC CHEDDAR MUFFINS

SHRIMP AND CORN BISQUE

CREAMY VEGETABLE SOUP

and cook until chicken is tender (about 45 minutes). Remove chicken and cool for 10 minutes. Pull chicken from bones, and chop into bite-size pieces; cover and refrigerate until ready to use. Strain broth, discarding solids and set aside.

2. In a Dutch oven over medium-high heat, combine flour and oil. Whisking constantly, cook for 15 to 20 minutes until flour mixture turns dark brown. Add onion, bell pepper, celery, and sausage, stirring to mix well. Add reserved chicken broth, and stir until well combined. Bring to a boil; reduce heat to medium-low, and cook, uncovered, for 1½ hours, stirring occasionally.

3. Add chicken, and cook for 15 minutes. Remove from heat, and let stand for 5 minutes. Skim surface to remove any fat. Stir in green onion and parsley, and serve with hot cooked rice.

4. Garnish with chopped red bell pepper, chopped parsley, hot sauce, and ground red pepper, if desired.

Garlic Cheddar Muffins
Makes 1 dozen

1   tablespoon olive oil
¼   cup butter
¼   cup chopped fresh chives
1½ teaspoons minced garlic
2   cups all-purpose baking mix
1   cup grated extra-sharp Cheddar cheese
¼   teaspoon garlic powder
¼   teaspoon ground black pepper
1   cup buttermilk

1. Preheat oven to 350°. Grease a 12-cup muffin pan with olive oil.

2. In a small saucepan, melt butter over medium heat. Add chives and garlic, and cook for 2 minutes; remove from heat, and set aside.

3. In a medium bowl, combine baking mix, cheese, garlic powder, and pepper.

4. In a separate bowl, combine buttermilk and butter mixture. Add buttermilk mixture to baking mixture, stirring until dry ingredients are moistened. Let batter stand for 5 minutes. Evenly spoon batter into prepared muffin pan. Bake for 30 minutes until golden brown. Cool in pan for 5 minutes before removing.

Chicken and Andouille Gumbo
Makes 10 to 12 servings

12 cups water
4   skinless bone-in chicken breasts
3   stalks celery, cut into large pieces
2   medium yellow onions, quartered
3   bay leaves
1   tablespoon salt
1   tablespoon Creole seasoning
1½ cups all-purpose flour
1½ cups vegetable oil
2   cups diced yellow onion
½   cup chopped green bell pepper
½   cup chopped red bell pepper
1   cup chopped celery
2   pounds andouille sausage, cut into
      ½-inch slices
¼   cup chopped green onion
¼   cup chopped fresh parsley
Hot cooked rice
Garnish: chopped red bell pepper, chopped fresh
      parsley, hot sauce, ground red pepper

1. In a heavy-duty Dutch oven over high heat, combine water, chicken, celery, onions, bay leaves, salt, and Creole seasoning, and bring to a boil. Reduce heat to medium,

for 4 minutes. Add onion, carrot, celery, salt, and pepper; sauté for 5 minutes.

2. Add sherry; cook for 2 minutes. Add tomato paste and garlic; cook for 2 to 3 minutes, stirring frequently. Add water and bay leaves; bring to a boil. Reduce heat to medium-low, and simmer for 45 minutes. Strain shrimp broth, discarding solids; set aside.

3. In a Dutch oven, melt butter over medium heat. Add flour, and cook for 3 minutes, stirring constantly. Add corn, and cook for 3 to 4 minutes, stirring constantly. Gradually add shrimp broth, whisking constantly until smooth. Bring to a boil; reduce heat to medium-low, and simmer for 35 minutes. Add cream, whisking constantly until smooth; cook for 2 minutes until just heated through.

4. In a large skillet, heat remaining 2 tablespoons oil over medium-high heat. Add shrimp, and sauté for 1 to 2 minutes on each side or just until shrimp turn pink. To serve, ladle bisque into bowls, and garnish with sautéed shrimp and parsley, if desired.

Creamy Vegetable Soup
Makes about 1½ quarts

2   tablespoons butter
2   tablespoons olive oil
1½ cups finely chopped onion
1   cup finely chopped celery
1   cup finely chopped carrot
1   (11-ounce) can corn, drained
2   teaspoons garlic powder
½   teaspoon salt
½   teaspoon ground black pepper
3   tablespoons all-purpose flour
1   quart chicken broth
1   cup heavy whipping cream
Garnish: chopped celery, chopped carrot, fresh parsley

1. In a medium saucepan, heat butter and olive oil over medium heat until butter is melted. Add onion, celery, carrot, and corn. Cook for 5 minutes, stirring frequently. Stir in garlic powder, salt, and pepper until well combined. Add flour, and cook for 2 minutes, stirring constantly.

2. Gradually add chicken broth, stirring to mix well. Bring to a simmer, stirring occasionally. Add cream, and cook for 15 to 20 minutes until soup thickens slightly. Top each serving with chopped celery, chopped carrot, and fresh parsley, if desired.

Shrimp and Corn Bisque
Makes 2½ quarts

1½ pounds large shrimp
¼   cup plus 2 tablespoons olive oil, divided
1½ cups chopped onion
¾   cup chopped carrot
¾   cup chopped celery
1   tablespoon salt
¾   teaspoon ground black pepper
1   cup dry sherry
3   tablespoons tomato paste
3   garlic cloves, minced
2   quarts water
6   bay leaves
½   cup butter
½   cup flour
2   cups frozen cream-style corn
1   cup heavy whipping cream
Garnish: chopped fresh parsley

1. Peel and devein shrimp, reserving shells. Cover and refrigerate shrimp for later use. In a Dutch oven, heat ¼ cup oil over medium-high heat. Add shrimp shells; sauté

MENU

GARLIC BREAD

ROASTED FALL VEGETABLES

SAVORY GREEN BEANS

ROASTED TURKEY WITH
GARLIC-LEMON BUTTER

SWEET POTATO
GINGERBREAD WITH MAPLE
PECAN BUTTER SAUCE

Gracious THANKSGIVING

·

Every November, grateful hearts take a day to pause, join hands around the harvest table, and give thanks together with family. Hearty fall flavors and delectable desserts signal the start of the holiday season. Look to the bounty of the fields to inspire a farm-to-table celebration that is both delicious and beautiful.

Garlic Bread
Makes 10 to 12 servings

3　heads garlic, unpeeled
2　tablespoons olive oil
½　cup butter, softened
2　tablespoons chopped fresh parsley
1　teaspoon fresh lemon juice
1　teaspoon crushed red pepper flakes (optional)
1　large loaf French bread, sliced in half lengthwise

1. Preheat oven to 425°. Cut tops off garlic heads. Place garlic on aluminum foil. Drizzle garlic with olive oil. Fold edges of foil together to seal. Bake for 30 minutes; let cool.
2. Reduce heat to 375°.
3. Squeeze cooked garlic into a small bowl. Add butter, parsley, lemon juice, and red pepper flakes, if desired, stirring to mix well. Spread both halves of bread with butter mixture. Bake for 15 to 20 minutes or until bread is lightly browned. Serve warm.

Tip: If you like a little heat, sprinkle with crushed red pepper flakes.

Roasted Fall Vegetables
Makes 6 to 8 servings

4　carrots, peeled and sliced to ½-inch thickness
4　parsnips, peeled and sliced to ½-inch thickness
1　sweet potato, peeled and diced to ½-inch thickness
1　butternut squash, peeled and diced to ½-inch thickness
1　(10-ounce) bag red or white pearl onions, peeled
6　tablespoons olive oil
2　tablespoons chopped fresh rosemary
1¾　teaspoons salt
½　teaspoon ground black pepper

1. Preheat oven to 450°. Line a rimmed baking sheet with aluminum foil; set aside.
2. In a large bowl, combine vegetables.
3. In a small bowl, combine olive oil, rosemary, salt, and pepper. Add olive-oil mixture to vegetables, tossing to coat evenly.
4. Spoon coated vegetables in an even layer onto prepared baking sheet. Bake for 20 minutes or until tender, stirring halfway through cooking time. Increase heat to broil. Broil for 4 to 5 minutes.

Savory Green Beans
Makes 10 to 12 servings

8   quarts water
1   tablespoon salt
3   pounds small green beans, washed and trimmed
3   tablespoons fresh lemon juice
2½ teaspoons garlic salt
¼   teaspoon ground black pepper
¼   cup olive oil
Garnish: lemon slices

1. Preheat oven to 450°. Line a large rimmed baking sheet with aluminum foil.
2. In a large Dutch oven or stockpot, combine water and salt. Bring to a boil over medium-high heat. Add green beans, and cook until just tender, 8 to 10 minutes. Drain, rinse with cold water, and drain again.
3. In a large bowl, combine lemon juice, garlic salt, and pepper; whisk in olive oil until well blended. Add green beans, and toss to coat completely; place in prepared pan. Bake for 25 to 30 minutes, stirring every 10 minutes. Garnish with lemon slices, if desired.

Roasted Turkey with Garlic-Lemon Butter
Makes 8 to 10 servings

1   cup butter, room temperature
2   tablespoons chopped fresh garlic
2   tablespoons fresh lemon juice
1½ teaspoons salt
1   teaspoon ground black pepper
1   (16- to 18-pound) whole turkey
Garnish: fresh rosemary sprigs, fresh thyme sprigs

1. Preheat oven to 325°.
2. In a medium bowl, combine butter, garlic, lemon juice, salt, and pepper. Rub butter mxture on skin and in cavity of turkey. Truss turkey with butcher's twine. Place turkey, breast side up, on a rack in a roasting pan. Cover with foil. Bake for 3 hours.
3. Remove foil, and bake 1 hour longer or until a meat thermometer inserted into the thigh registers 180°, basting occasionally with pan juices. Remove turkey from oven, and let stand for 10 minutes. Garnish with rosemary and thyme, if desired. Serve with pan juices.

Tip: You will find fresh rosemary and thyme in your grocer's produce section.

Sweet Potato Gingerbread with Maple Pecan Butter Sauce
Makes 12 servings

2½ cups all-purpose flour
1½ teaspoons baking soda
1½ teaspoons ground ginger
1   teaspoon baking powder
1   teaspoon salt
½   teaspoon ground cinnamon
1¼ cups firmly packed light brown sugar
½   cup butter, softened
1   cup mashed cooked sweet potato
½   cup evaporated milk
¼   cup dark molasses
2   large eggs
1   teaspoon vanilla extract
Maple Pecan Butter Sauce (recipe follows)

1. Preheat oven to 350°. Grease and flour a 13x9-inch pan.
2. In a medium bowl, sift together flour, baking soda, ginger, baking powder, salt, and cinnamon; set aside.
3. In a large bowl, combine brown sugar and butter; beat at medium speed with an electric mixer until fluffy. Add sweet potato, milk, molasses, eggs, and vanilla, beating to mix well. Gradually add flour mixture to sweet potato mixture, beating until combined.
4. Spoon batter into prepared pan. Bake for 30 to 40 minutes or until a wooden pick inserted in center comes out clean. Let cool in pan for 10 minutes. Remove from pan, and cut into 12 squares. Serve warm with Maple Pecan Butter Sauce.

Maple Pecan Butter Sauce
Makes about 2 cups

1   cup maple syrup
½   cup butter, cut into pieces
¼   cup sugar
1   large egg, lightly beaten
1   tablespoon vanilla extract
1   cup pecan pieces

1. In a medium saucepan, combine maple syrup, butter, sugar, and egg over medium heat. Simmer mixture for 6 minutes, whisking constantly. Remove from heat, and stir in vanilla. Just before serving, stir in pecans. Serve warm.

Thanksgiving Simplicity

Heirloom pumpkins, with their varied tones and patterns, put a new spin on the classic orange. Capture this theme by mixing and matching a rainbow of solid harvest-colored dishes at each place setting. Place your linens, patterned place mats, and napkins atop a neutral, solid-colored tablecloth.

Fall

Just DESSERTS

Peanut Butter Thumbprint Cookies
Makes about 4 dozen

1   cup firmly packed light brown sugar
¾   cup peanut butter
½   cup butter, softened
2   large eggs
1   teaspoon vanilla extract
2¼ cups all-purpose flour
1   teaspoon baking soda
¼   teaspoon salt
2   cups semisweet chocolate morsels

1. Preheat oven to 375°. Line baking sheets with parchment paper; set aside.
2. In a large bowl, combine brown sugar, peanut butter, and butter. Beat at medium speed with an electric mixer until fluffy. Add eggs and vanilla, beating until well combined. In a medium bowl, combine flour, baking soda, and salt. Add flour mixture to sugar mixture, beating until well combined.
3. Shape dough into 1-inch balls. Place 2 inches apart on prepared baking sheets. Using your thumb, make an indentation in center of each cookie. Bake for 7 minutes. Remove from oven; press indentation again. Return to oven, and bake for 1 to 2 minutes longer, or until set. Let cool on pans 2 minutes. Remove from pan, and let cool completely on wire racks.
4. In a small microwave-safe bowl, microwave chocolate morsels on High in 30-second intervals, stirring between each, until chocolate is melted and smooth (about 1 minute total). Spoon about 1 teaspoon melted chocolate into center of each cookie. Let stand until set.

Pecan Date Cookies
Makes about 4 dozen

3   cups all-purpose flour
1½ teaspoons baking powder
¼   teaspoon salt
¼   teaspoon ground cinnamon
¼   teaspoon ground nutmeg
¼   teaspoon ground cloves
1   cup unsalted butter, softened
1   cup plus 2 tablespoons sugar, divided
½   cup firmly packed light brown sugar
2   large eggs
1   teaspoon vanilla extract
2½ cups chopped pecans
2½ cups chopped dates

1. Preheat oven to 325°. Line baking sheets with parchment paper.
2. In a medium bowl, combine flour, baking powder, salt, cinnamon, nutmeg, and cloves.
3. In a separate bowl, combine butter, 1 cup sugar, and brown sugar. Beat at medium speed with an electric mixer until fluffy. Add eggs and vanilla; beat until well combined. Gradually add flour mixture to butter mixture, beating until dry ingredients are moistened. Stir in pecans and dates. Drop by rounded teaspoonfuls onto prepared baking sheets. Sprinkle with remaining 2 tablespoons sugar. Bake for 20 to 22 minutes or until lightly browned. Cool on pans for 2 minutes; remove to wire racks, and cool completely.

" I am beginning to learn that it is the sweet, simple things of life which are the real ones after all."

—Laura Ingalls Wilder

Winter

Outside, Nature has adorned herself with a glittering display of
frost and icicles. Inside, the warmth of merry hearts and holiday cheer
melts away the chill, leaving only the festive sparkle of the winter
season paired with the regal glow of celebration.

MENU

HOT PIMIENTO CHEESE DIP

ROASTED ZUCCHINI
AND CARROTS

TURKEY WITH ORANGE
ROSEMARY GLAZE

SNOWFLAKE CAKE WITH
EGGNOG FROSTING

Southern
CHRISTMAS

·

When a chill is in the air and frost is on the ground, nothing warms the heart and soul more than joining with family and friends to celebrate the Christmas season. Food and decorating trends may come and go, but your guests will always appreciate a timeless red and green Christmas motif with all the traditional trimmings.

Hot Pimiento Cheese Dip
Makes 8 to 10 servings

1   (8-ounce) block extra-sharp Cheddar cheese,
    shredded
1   (8-ounce) block Monterey Jack cheese, shredded
1   (7-ounce) jar diced pimientos, drained
½   cup mayonnaise
¼   cup sour cream
1   teaspoon Worcestershire sauce
½   teaspoon ground red pepper

1. Preheat oven to 350°.
2. In a medium bowl, combine cheeses, pimientos, mayonnaise, sour cream, Worcestershire sauce, and red pepper, stirring to combine well. Spoon cheese mixture into a
1-quart baking dish. Bake for 20 minutes or until bubbly.
Serve with pita chips or crackers.

Roasted Zucchini and Carrots
Makes 8 to 10 servings

2   pounds carrots, peeled and sliced to ½-inch thickness
4   large zucchini, halved lengthwise and sliced into
    ½-inch thickness
3   tablespoons olive oil
2   tablespoons chopped fresh thyme
1   teaspoon salt
¾   teaspoon ground black pepper
¾   teaspoon granulated garlic

1. Preheat oven to 450°. Line a rimmed baking sheet with
aluminum foil.
2. In a large bowl, combine carrots, zucchini, olive oil,
thyme, salt, pepper, and granulated garlic, tossing to coat
evenly. Bake for 25 to 30 minutes or until tender, stirring
halfway through cooking time.

Turkey with Orange Rosemary Glaze
Makes 8 to 10 servings

1   (12- to 14-pound) whole turkey, washed, giblets
    removed
2   tablespoons olive oil
1½ teaspoons salt
1   teaspoon ground black pepper
2   oranges, sliced to ½-inch thickness
1   (1-ounce) package fresh rosemary
Orange Rosemary Glaze (recipe follows)
Garnish: orange wedges, fresh rosemary

(continued on page 81)

1. Preheat oven to 325°. Rub surface of turkey with olive oil. Sprinkle with salt and pepper.

2. Place orange slices and rosemary inside of turkey. Truss turkey with butcher's twine. Place, breast side up, on a rack in a roasting pan. Cover with foil, and bake for 3 hours.

3. Remove foil, and bake 1 hour longer or until a meat thermometer inserted in the thigh registers 180° and juices run clear. Baste turkey with glaze during last hour of roasting. Remove pan from oven, and let stand for 10 minutes before slicing. Garnish with orange wedges and fresh rosemary, if desired.

Orange Rosemary Glaze
Makes about 1½ cups

1   tablespoon orange zest
2   cups fresh orange juice
½   cup orange marmalade
3   tablespoons soy sauce
2   tablespoons Dijon mustard
1   tablespoon chopped fresh rosemary
½   teaspoon salt
¼   teaspoon ground black pepper

1. In a medium saucepan, combine orange zest, orange juice, marmalade, soy sauce, Dijon mustard, rosemary, salt, and pepper over medium heat. Bring to a simmer; cook, uncovered, for 20 minutes or until mixture thickens slightly.

Snowflake Cake with Eggnog Frosting
Makes 1 (3-layer) cake

1   cup butter, softened
1   cup sugar
1   cup firmly packed light brown sugar
1   teaspoon vanilla extract
6   large eggs
3   cups cake flour
1   teaspoon baking powder
½   teaspoon baking soda
½   teaspoon ground nutmeg
¼   teaspoon salt
1½   cups prepared eggnog
Eggnog Frosting (recipe follows)

1. Preheat oven to 350°. Grease and flour 3 (8-inch) round cake pans.

2. In a large bowl, beat butter and sugars at medium speed with an electric mixer until fluffy. Add vanilla, beating to combine. Add eggs, one at a time, beating well after each addition.

3. In a medium bowl, sift together flour, baking powder, baking soda, nutmeg, and salt. Gradually add flour mixture to butter mixture alternately with eggnog, beginning and ending with flour mixture. Spoon batter into prepared pans. Bake for 25 to 30 minutes or until a wooden pick inserted in centers comes out clean. Let cool in pans for 10 minutes.

4. Remove cakes from pans, and let cool completely on wire racks. Spread Eggnog Frosting between layers and on top and sides of cake.

Eggnog Frosting
Makes 5½ cups

½   cup butter, softened
8   cups confectioners' sugar, sifted
½   cup prepared eggnog
¾   teaspoon ground nutmeg

1. In a large bowl, beat butter at medium speed with an electric mixer until creamy. Gradually add confectioners' sugar alternately with eggnog, beating until smooth. Add nutmeg, beating until well combined.

Jolly Feast

Start with the basics, and add Christmas spirit with your accessories. Stretch your holiday china by pairing your patterned plates with plain white plates. Ribbon-wrap basic accessories like white pillar candles and napkins to give them a festive makeover. Tiny sleigh ornaments serve as both favor and place card holder.

Shining
NEW YEAR

*Celebrate the memories of the past year, and anticipate the promise
of the new. Rich purples and sparkling accents shimmer in the
candlelight of this festive party, while the traditional lucky fare of
black-eyed peas rings in hopes for a prosperous New Year.*

MENU

FONTINA GRITS CAKES WITH
CHIPOTLE SHRIMP AND
CILANTRO CREAM

SPARKLING
POMEGRANATE COCKTAIL

SAUTÉED COLLARDS

PIMIENTO CHEESE RICE

PORK MEDALLIONS WITH
BLACK-EYED PEA RELISH

CINNAMON-ORANGE
POUND CAKE

aluminum foil. Brush foil with melted butter; set aside.

4. Unmold grits onto a large cutting board. Using a 2¼-inch round cutter, cut out 18 circles. Place grits rounds on prepared sheet. Bake for 30 minutes, turning halfway through cooking time.

5. In a medium bowl, combine ketchup, adobo sauce, garlic, cumin, chili powder, and salt. Add shrimp, tossing gently to coat; let stand for 5 minutes.

6. In a large nonstick skillet, heat olive oil over medium heat. Add shrimp; cook for 1 to 2 minutes on each side or until shrimp are firm. Spoon Cilantro Cream on top of each grits cake; top with shrimp. Garnish with fresh cilantro, if desired.

Cilantro Cream
Makes about 1 cup

1   (8-ounce) container sour cream
3   tablespoons chopped fresh cilantro
2   tablespoons finely chopped green onion
¼   teaspoon salt
¼   teaspoon garlic powder
⅛   teaspoon ground red pepper

1. In a small bowl, combine sour cream, cilantro, green onion, salt, garlic powder, and red pepper.

Sautéed Collards
Makes 8 servings

3   quarts water
2   (1-pound) bags chopped collard greens
¼   cup olive oil
1   large yellow onion, thinly sliced
1   tablespoon minced garlic
¾   cup chicken broth
¼   cup balsamic vinegar
2   teaspoons sugar
1½   teaspoons salt
1   teaspoon crushed red pepper flakes
½   teaspoon garlic powder

1. In a large Dutch oven, bring water to a boil. Add collards; cook for 3 minutes, stirring occasionally. Remove from heat, and drain thoroughly; set aside.

2. In Dutch oven, heat olive oil over medium-high heat. Add onion; cook for 5 to 6 minutes, stirring constantly, until lightly browned. Add garlic; cook for 1 minute, stirring constantly. Add collards; cook for 2 minutes, stirring frequently. Add chicken broth, vinegar, sugar, salt, red pepper flakes, and garlic powder. Cook for 5 minutes, stirring frequently.

Fontina Grits Cakes with Chipotle Shrimp
Makes 1½ dozen

3¼   cups chicken broth
1½   cups quick-cooking grits
1   cup finely grated fontina cheese
¼   teaspoon salt
¼   teaspoon ground black pepper
Cilantro Cream (recipe follows)
2   tablespoons butter, melted
¼   cup ketchup
1½   tablespoons adobo sauce
2   teaspoons minced garlic
1   teaspoon ground cumin
1   teaspoon chili powder
½   teaspoon salt
18   fresh jumbo shrimp, peeled and deveined (tails left on)
2   tablespoons olive oil
Garnish: fresh cilantro

1. Line a 13x9-inch baking pan with parchment paper; set aside.

2. In a large saucepan, bring chicken broth to a boil. Stir in grits, and return to a boil. Cover, reduce heat, and simmer for 5 minutes or until grits are thickened, stirring occasionally. Add cheese, salt, and pepper, stirring until cheese is melted. Spoon grits into prepared pan; let cool for 5 minutes. Cover and chill for 2 hours or until firm. Prepare Cilantro Cream; cover and chill.

3. Preheat oven to 400°. Line a rimmed baking sheet with

Sparkling Pomegranate Cocktail
Makes 1 drink

1½ ounces pomegranate juice
1   ounce pomegranate syrup
1   ounce pomegranate liqueur
4   ounces chilled Champagne
Garnish: pomegranate seeds

1. In a chilled Champagne flute, combine pomegranate juice, pomegranate syrup, and pomegranate liqueur. Add Champagne. Garnish with pomegranate seeds, if desired.

Tip: Visit *torani.com* to find sources for the pomegranate-flavored syrup.

Pork Medallions with Black-Eyed Pea Relish

Makes 8 servings

3   (1-pound) pork tenderloins, trimmed
1½ cups all-purpose flour
1½ tablespoons seasoned salt
1   teaspoon ground black pepper
1   teaspoon garlic powder
Olive oil for frying
Black-Eyed Pea Relish (recipe follows)

1. Cut tenderloins into 2-ounce pieces. Place pork between 2 sheets of plastic wrap; pound with a meat mallet to ¼-inch thickness.
2. In a shallow dish, combine flour, seasoned salt, pepper, and garlic powder. Coat pork medallions in flour mixture, shaking off excess.
3. In a large skillet, pour olive oil to a ⅛-inch depth. Heat olive oil over medium heat. Cook pork for 2 to 3 minutes on each side or until golden brown. Serve with Black-Eyed Pea Relish.

Black-Eyed Pea Relish

Makes about 4 cups

⅓   cup apple-cider vinegar
3   tablespoons firmly packed light brown sugar
2   tablespoons olive oil
2   teaspoons mustard seed
¾   teaspoon celery salt
½   teaspoon salt
½   teaspoon ground black pepper
¼   teaspoon ground red pepper
2   (15.8-ounce) cans black-eyed peas, rinsed and drained
1   cup seeded and chopped tomato
½   cup chopped red bell pepper
½   cup chopped celery
½   cup chopped green onion
1   tablespoon chopped fresh parsley

1. In a medium saucepan, combine vinegar, brown sugar, olive oil, mustard seed, celery salt, salt, black pepper, and red pepper over medium heat. Cook for 2 minutes, stirring until brown sugar is dissolved. Add black-eyed peas, tomato, bell pepper, celery, green onion, and parsley, stirring to combine well. Cook for 2 to 3 minutes, stirring occasionally, just until heated through.

Pimiento Cheese Rice

Makes 8 servings

5   tablespoons butter
4   teaspoons minced garlic
1   (15-ounce) jar roasted red peppers, drained and chopped
3   cups uncooked basmati rice
6   cups chicken broth
1   teaspoon salt
½   teaspoon ground black pepper
2   cups shredded Cheddar cheese
½   cup heavy whipping cream

1. In a large saucepan, heat butter over medium heat until melted. Add garlic and red peppers; cook for 2 minutes, stirring frequently. Add rice; cook for 2 to 3 minutes, stirring constantly. Add chicken broth, salt, and pepper. Bring to a boil; reduce heat to medium-low, and simmer, covered, for 20 to 25 minutes or until liquid is absorbed. Fluff rice with a fork. Add cheese and cream, stirring until cheese is melted.

Tip: Sometimes referred to as "Southern pâté," pimiento cheese adds flavor and color to a rice side dish.

Cinnamon-Orange Pound Cake

Makes 10 to 12 servings

¾ cup butter, softened
¾ cup shortening
3 cups sugar
2 tablespoons orange zest
2 teaspoons ground cinnamon
1½ teaspoons vanilla extract
7 large eggs
3 cups all-purpose flour
¼ teaspoon salt
¾ cup milk
Garnish: candied orange slices

1. Preheat oven to 300°. Spray a tube pan with nonstick baking spray with flour. Line pan with parchment paper.
2. In a large bowl, beat butter, shortening, sugar, orange zest, cinnamon, and vanilla at medium speed with an electric mixer until fluffy. Add eggs, one at a time, beating well after each addition.
3. In a small bowl, sift together flour and salt. Gradually add flour mixture to butter mixture alternately with milk, beating to mix well. Spoon batter into prepared pan. Bake for 1 hour. Cover loosely with aluminum foil, and bake 45 to 50 minutes longer. Cool cake in pan for 10 minutes. Remove to wire rack, and let cool completely. Garnish with candied orange slices, if desired.

*"Ring out the old,
ring in the new,
Ring, happy bells,
across the snow:*

*The year is going,
let him go;
Ring out the false,
ring in the true."*

—Alfred Lord Tennyson

MENU

**VALENTINE HEART SALAD
WITH CREAMY BALSAMIC
ITALIAN DRESSING**

**PASTA WITH MUSHROOMS
AND ROASTED GARLIC**

VEAL PICCATA

SWEETHEART TARTS

Candlelight DINNER

·

It's the most romantic time of the year. Skip the restaurant crowds, and cuddle up with your sweetheart at home for a romantic celebration. Keep the decorations simple with heart-capturing elegant roses and sentimental décor for your table so you can spend more time focusing on your Valentine.

Valentine Heart Salad
Makes 2 servings

4   cups torn green leaf lettuce
1   cup small artichoke hearts, halved
2   hearts of palm, sliced
½   cup chopped prosciutto
Creamy Balsamic Italian Dressing (recipe follows)
Garnish: toasted pine nuts, shaved Parmigiano-
    Reggiano cheese

1. Divide lettuce, artichoke hearts, hearts of palm, and prosciutto evenly between 2 salad plates. Drizzle with Creamy Balsamic Italian Dressing just before serving. Garnish with toasted pine nuts and cheese, if desired.

Creamy Balsamic Italian Dressing
Makes about 1 cup

¾   cup mayonnaise
¼   cup buttermilk
¼   cup balsamic vinegar
1   tablespoon Italian seasoning
½   teaspoon sugar
¼   teaspoon garlic salt
¼   teaspoon ground black pepper

1. In a small bowl, combine all ingredients, whisking until smooth. Cover and chill until ready to serve.

Pasta with Mushrooms and Roasted Garlic
Makes 2 servings

2   tablespoons butter
2   tablespoons olive oil
1   (8-ounce) container sliced baby bella mushrooms
½   cup chopped leek
¼   cup dry white wine
1   tablespoon chopped roasted garlic
3   cups cooked fettuccine noodles
2   tablespoons chopped fresh basil
½   teaspoon salt
¼   teaspoon ground black pepper
Garnish: freshly grated Parmigiano-Reggiano cheese,
    fresh basil

1. In a large sauté pan, heat butter and olive oil over medium heat until butter is melted. Add mushrooms and leek; cook for 7 to 8 minutes. Add wine and roasted garlic; cook for 1 minute, stirring constantly. Add fettuccine, basil, salt, and pepper; toss gently to combine. Garnish with cheese and fresh basil, if desired.

Veal Piccata
Makes 2 servings

½   cup all-purpose flour
½   teaspoon salt
¼   teaspoon ground black pepper
½   pound veal cutlets
4   tablespoons butter, divided
2   tablespoons olive oil
2   tablespoons capers
2   teaspoons minced garlic
½   cup chicken broth
¼   cup dry white wine
¼   cup fresh lemon juice
1   tablespoon chopped fresh parsley

1. In a shallow dish, combine flour, salt, and pepper. Coat veal cutlets in flour mixture, shaking off excess.
2. In a large nonstick skillet, heat 2 tablespoons butter and olive oil over medium-high heat, until butter is melted. Cook veal for 1½ to 2 minutes on each side or until golden brown. Remove from heat; place veal in a warm oven (200°).
3. Add capers and garlic to skillet over medium heat; cook for 1 minute. Add chicken broth, wine, and lemon juice; cook for 4 minutes, stirring frequently. Add remaining 2 tablespoons butter and parsley. Cook, stirring until butter *(Continued on page 95)*

is melted and sauce has thickened slightly, about 1 minute. Remove from heat. Serve veal with desired amount of sauce.

Sweetheart Tarts
Makes 4 servings

½   (14.1-ounce) package refrigerated pie crusts
1   (3-ounce) package cream cheese, softened
2   tablespoons seedless raspberry preserves
2   tablespoons confectioners' sugar
1   tablespoon raspberry-flavored liqueur
½   cup semisweet chocolate morsels
2   tablespoons heavy whipping cream
1   teaspoon light corn syrup, divided
Garnish: fresh raspberries, chocolate curls

1. Preheat oven to 450°. Spray 4 (3½-inch) heart-shaped tart pans with nonstick cooking spray; set aside.
2. On a lightly floured surface, unroll crust. Using a 4¼-inch round cutter, cut 4 circles from pie crust. Line prepared pans with crusts; crimp edges, if desired. Prick bottoms of crusts with a fork. Place on a baking sheet; bake for 10 to 12 minutes, or until golden brown. Let cool in pans for 2 minutes. Remove from pans, and let cool completely on a wire rack.
3. In a small bowl, combine cream cheese, raspberry preserves, confectioners' sugar, and liqueur. Beat at medium speed with an electric mixer until smooth; set aside.
4. In a separate small bowl, combine chocolate morsels, cream, and corn syrup. Microwave on High, in 30-second intervals, stirring between each, until chocolate is melted and smooth (about 1 minute total). Spread cream cheese mixture into the bottoms of tart shells. Spread chocolate mixture over cream cheese mixture. To serve, garnish with fresh raspberries and chocolate curls, if desired.

Tip: Chocolate curls can be purchased, if desired, from specialty and gourmet markets. To make your own, use a vegetable peeler to shave thin wisps or curls along the side of a room-temperature chocolate bar. Refrigerate the curls until ready to use.

Table for Two

Turn your coffee table into a dining table for your cozy and romantic fireside evening. If it's too warm outside to light a fire, set the mood with a profusion of candles on the hearth. Red roses defy cliché when paired with unusual items like textural twigs and berries.

Just DESSERTS

Apple Pear Cranberry Pie
Makes 1 (9½-inch) pie

4   cups thinly sliced Granny Smith
    apples
3   cups thinly sliced green Anjou
    pears
1   cup dried cranberries
2   tablespoons fresh lemon juice
⅔   cup firmly packed brown sugar
¼   cup plus 1 tablespoon sugar,
    divided
¼   cup cornstarch
½   teaspoon ground cinnamon
¼   teaspoon ground nutmeg
⅛   teaspoon salt
Double Crust Pie Pastry (recipe follows)
1   tablespoon milk

1. Preheat oven to 350°.
2. In a large bowl, combine apples, pears, cranberries, and lemon juice. Toss gently to coat; set aside.
3. In a separate bowl, combine brown sugar, ¼ cup sugar, cornstarch, cinnamon, nutmeg, and salt. Combine brown sugar mixture with apple mixture; toss gently to coat.
4. On a lightly floured surface, roll half of pastry to a 12-inch circle. Place in a 9½-inch deep-dish pie plate. Trim excess pastry ½ inch beyond edge of pie plate. Place apple mixture into prepared crust. Roll remaining pastry to ⅛-inch thickness. Using a pastry wheel or knife, cut into ½-inch-wide strips. Arrange in lattice design over apple mixture. Trim strips even with edges. Press edges of crust together. Fold edges under, and crimp. Brush crust with milk, and sprinkle with remaining 1 tablespoon sugar. Bake for 45 to 50 minutes or until lightly browned.

Double Crust Pie Pastry
Makes 1 double pie crust

3   cups all-purpose flour
1   teaspoon salt
⅔   cup shortening
7   tablespoons cold water

1. In a medium bowl, combine flour and salt. Using a pastry blender, cut in shortening until mixture is crumbly. Add water, and stir just until moistened. Divide dough into 2 balls. Wrap tightly in plastic wrap; refrigerate for 1 hour.

Party Petits Fours
Makes about 2 dozen petits fours

2   (16-ounce) frozen pound cakes,
    thawed
Lemon Filling (recipe follows)
1   (1½-pound) package vanilla
    candy coating or almond bark
½ to 1 block paraffin
Garnish: sliced almonds, candied
    lemon zest

1. Trim outer crust from pound cakes. Slice each horizontally into 3 even layers. With a 2-inch square cutter or knife, slice pound cakes into even squares.
2. Spread Lemon Filling between two layers of pound cake, and sandwich together. Place on a baking sheet, and freeze for 1 hour.
3. Melt candy coating and paraffin in microwave or double boiler. With a skewer, dip each sandwich to coat. Place on baking rack with waxed paper underneath. Allow to dry.
4. Garnish with a small dollop of candy coating, almonds, and candied lemon zest, if desired.

Lemon Filling
Makes 1 cup

5   egg yolks
¾   cup sugar
2   teaspoons lemon zest
⅓   cup fresh lemon juice
½   cup heavy whipping cream
½   teaspoon vanilla extract
½   cup unsalted butter,
    cut into pieces

1. In the top of double boiler, whisk together egg yolks, sugar, lemon zest, and lemon juice until blended.
2. Over simmering water, cook mixture for 7 to 8 minutes, whisking constantly, until thickened. Add cream; cook for 2 minutes.
3. Remove from heat; add vanilla. Whisk in butter, 1 tablespoon at a time.
4. Cover with plastic wrap, touching the surface of filling to prevent skin from forming. Store, covered, up to 1 month in refrigerator.

Celebrations

Every day of the year enjoyed with the love of family and friends is cause for joy, but some milestones are to be marked with special attention and celebration. Whether you are toasting a bride-to-be or welcoming a new baby, there's plenty of party ideas for every occasion.

MENU

STRAWBERRY LEMON PUNCH

CUCUMBER TEA SANDWICHES

Sugar and SPICE

·

Help the expectant Mommy welcome her pretty little one into the world with a shower that takes the cake. Joyful thrills, tasty treats, and adorable gifts will add to the already exciting time!

Strawberry Lemon Punch
Makes about 1 gallon

4 (10-ounce) packages frozen sliced strawberries in syrup, thawed and puréed
1 (12-ounce) can frozen lemonade concentrate, thawed
½ cup fresh lemon juice
1 (2-liter) bottle lemon-lime-flavored carbonated beverage, chilled
Garnish: fresh strawberries, lemon slices

1. In a 1-gallon pitcher, combine strawberry purée, lemonade concentrate, and lemon juice.
2. To serve, add lemon-lime-flavored beverage, and stir gently. Garnish with fresh strawberries and lemon slices, if desired.

Cucumber Tea Sandwiches
Makes about 3 dozen

1 (8-ounce) package cream cheese, softened
2 tablespoons mayonnaise
¾ teaspoon seasoned salt
¼ cup finely grated carrot
¼ cup finely chopped toasted walnuts
1 tablespoon finely chopped fresh parsley
1 seedless cucumber
12 pieces thinly sliced white sandwich bread, crusts removed
Garnish: finely grated carrot

1. In a small bowl, combine cream cheese, mayonnaise, and seasoned salt. Stir in carrot, walnuts, and parsley.
2. Using a vegetable peeler, peel thin ribbons of cucumber.
3. Spread a thin layer of cream cheese mixture onto bread. Place cucumber slices in a single layer, overlapping slightly, over cream cheese mixture. Cut each sandwich into thirds. Garnish with finely grated carrot, if desired.

Baby Bunting

For a look that won't go out of style, pepper your setting with classic designs like polka dots and gingham. Spoons, rattles, cups, and other silver baby items add charm, while stuffed animals and blankets can serve the dual purpose of gift and décor.

MENU

GREEN GODDESS DIP

**BACON PECAN
CHEESE WAFERS**

Snips and SNAILS

Help a mom prepare for the newest handsome little member of her family by showering her with love and a few fun gifts. Finger foods and fun animal accessories create the perfect backdrop for this celebration.

Green Goddess Dip
Makes 4 cups

2   (8-ounce) packages cream cheese, softened
1   (16-ounce) container sour cream
½   cup mayonnaise
3   tablespoons tarragon vinegar
6   tablespoons chopped fresh tarragon
6   tablespoons chopped green onion
6   tablespoons chopped fresh parsley
¼   cup chopped fresh chives
1½ teaspoons seasoned salt
1   teaspoon ground black pepper
¼   teaspoon garlic powder

1. In the work bowl of a food processor, combine cream cheese, sour cream, mayonnaise, and vinegar; process until smooth. Add tarragon, green onion, parsley, chives, seasoned salt, pepper, and garlic powder; process until smooth. Cover and refrigerate for 2 hours to overnight. Serve with fresh vegetables.

Bacon Pecan Cheese Wafers
Makes 7 dozen

1½ cups butter, softened
1   (1-pound) block sharp Cheddar cheese, finely grated
1   pound bacon, cooked and crumbled
1   cup finely chopped toasted pecans
½   cup finely chopped green onion
½   teaspoon ground red pepper
4½ cups all-purpose flour

1. In a large bowl, combine butter, cheese, bacon, pecans, green onion, and red pepper. Beat at medium speed with an electric mixer until well combined. Gradually add flour, beating until just combined. Wrap dough in plastic wrap, and refrigerate for 2 hours.
2. Preheat oven to 350°. Line baking sheets with parchment paper.
3. Roll dough into 1-inch balls. Place dough 3 inches apart on prepared baking sheets.
4. Lightly spray a flat-bottomed glass with nonstick cooking spray, and dip bottom of glass into flour. Using bottom of glass, flatten each dough ball to ¼-inch thickness, flouring glass as needed. Bake for 15 minutes or until lightly browned. Let cool on pans for 2 minutes. Remove from pans, and let cool completely on wire racks.

Mini Menagerie

Baby animals are the perfect motif for a little boy's shower. Stuffed animals and animal-themed accents like little lamb vases set the tone and add a playful whimsey to the setting. Use the white china serving pieces that you already own, and introduce the classic little boy blue through flowers and gift wrap.

Birthday
BREAKFAST

·

Make the birthday girl feel like a glamorous Hollywood socialite
with stunning breakfast fare, embellishments, and a showing
of the classic movie Breakfast at Tiffany's.

MENU

GOLIGHTLY AMBROSIA

GOAT-CHEESE-AND-
CHIVE SCONES

SALLY TOMATO RELISH

FRED BABY'S PECAN
WAFFLES WITH BANANAS
FOSTER TOPPING

HOLLY

Golightly Ambrosia
Makes 4 to 6 servings

6   navel oranges, sectioned
2   cups sliced strawberries
1   cup orange juice
2   tablespoons honey
1   tablespoon fresh lemon juice
¼   teaspoon ground cardamom
Garnish: toasted coconut flakes, toasted pistachios,
     strawberry halves

1. In a medium bowl, combine oranges and strawberries.
2. In a small bowl, combine orange juice, honey, lemon juice, and cardamom, whisking until honey dissolves. Pour orange juice mixture over fruit. Cover and refrigerate for 1 hour. Garnish with toasted coconut flakes, pistachios, and strawberry halves, if desired.

Goat-Cheese-and-Chive Scones
Makes about 1 dozen

3   cups self-rising flour
½   cup butter
2   (4-ounce) packages goat cheese
¼   cup finely minced chives
⅔   cup half-and-half
2   tablespoons butter, melted
Sally Tomato Relish (recipe follows)

1. Preheat oven to 425°. Line a baking sheet with parchment paper.
2. In a medium bowl, place flour. Using a pastry blender, cut in butter and goat cheese until mixture is crumbly. Add chives; stir well. Add half-and-half, stirring just until dry ingredients are moistened.
3. On a lightly floured surface, roll dough to ½-inch thickness. Cut scones, using a 2¾-inch heart-shaped cutter, and place on prepared sheet. Bake for 16 to 18 minutes or until lightly browned. Brush with melted butter. Serve with Sally Tomato Relish.

"Anyone who ever gave you confidence, you owe them a lot."

—Truman Capote, spoken by Holly Golightly,
Breakfast at Tiffany's

Sally Tomato Relish
Makes about 1½ cups

1   (35-ounce) can Italian plum tomatoes, drained
4   shallots, peeled
3   tablespoons unsulfured molasses,
     divided
2   tablespoons olive oil
¾   teaspoon salt, divided
½   teaspoon ground black pepper, divided
1   tablespoon balsamic vinegar

1. Preheat oven to 350°. Line a 13x9-inch rimmed baking sheet with heavy-duty aluminum foil.
2. Place tomatoes and shallots on prepared pan.
3. In a small bowl, combine 2 tablespoons molasses, olive oil, ½ teaspoon salt, and ¼ teaspoon pepper. Using a pastry brush, brush molasses mixture on both sides of tomatoes and shallots. Bake for 1 hour.
4. In the work bowl of a food processor, combine tomatoes, shallots, remaining 1 tablespoon molasses, ¼ teaspoon salt, ¼ teaspoon pepper, and vinegar. Pulse to desired consistency.

Fred Baby's Pecan Waffles with Bananas Foster Topping

Makes 1 dozen (4-inch) waffles

2   cups all-purpose flour
¼   cup sugar
1   teaspoon baking powder
1   teaspoon baking soda
½   teaspoon salt
½   cup finely chopped toasted pecans
3   large eggs
1¼   cups whole milk
½   cup sour cream
½   cup butter, melted
Bananas Foster Topping (recipe follows)

1. Preheat waffle iron.
2. In a medium bowl, combine flour, sugar, baking powder, baking soda, and salt. Stir in pecans.
3. In a separate bowl, whisk together eggs, milk, sour cream, and melted butter. Add egg mixture to flour mixture, whisking until smooth. Pour batter onto waffle iron, in batches, and cook until waffles are browned. Serve with Bananas Foster Topping.

Bananas Foster Topping

Makes 4 to 6 servings

¼   cup butter
¼   cup firmly packed dark brown sugar
½   teaspoon ground cinnamon
2   tablespoons banana schnapps
2   tablespoons dark rum
¼   cup cane syrup
3   large ripe bananas, peeled and sliced
¾   cup pecan halves

1. In a medium skillet, melt butter over low heat. Add brown sugar and cinnamon; cook for 3 to 4 minutes, stirring constantly, until sugar dissolves. Increase heat to medium; add banana schnapps and rum; cook for 3 minutes, stirring frequently. Add syrup; cook for 1 minute. Add bananas and pecans; cook for 2 minutes, stirring gently to coat bananas. Serve warm.

Stylish Look

Refined elegance rules the day with a simple palette of Tiffany blue and white. Classic white roses in milk glass and crystal vases pair prettily with the lustrous glow of silver serving pieces, and a sprinkling of pearl and rhinestone accents gives just the right amount of sparkle and shine to the celebration.

MENU

SPARKLING
RASPBERRY PUNCH

GRILLED CHICKEN SALAD

Blissful
BRIDE-TO-BE

Little girls have been known to dream about and even act out their wedding day. The envisioned moment is almost here for the beautiful bride-to-be. Host a tea for her that marks this wonderful celebration of love with a delicious menu and captivating accents.

Sparkling Raspberry Punch
Makes 14½ cups

1   (750-milliliter) bottle sparkling grape juice
1   (12-ounce) container frozen pink lemonade
     concentrate, thawed
1   (12-ounce) bottle raspberry syrup
1   (2-liter) bottle ginger ale, chilled
Garnish: fresh raspberries

1. In a large container, combine grape juice, pink lemon-ade concentrate, and raspberry syrup. To serve, gently stir in ginger ale. Garnish with fresh raspberries, if desired.

Tip: You may substitute Champagne for the sparkling grape juice.

Grilled Chicken Salad
Makes 6 servings

3   boneless, skinless chicken breasts
½   teaspoon kosher salt
½   teaspoon freshly ground black pepper
¼   cup Champagne vinegar
¾   cup extra-virgin olive oil
3   tablespoons coarse-grained mustard
2   tablespoons chopped fresh tarragon
1   tablespoon chopped fresh shallot
1   tablespoon minced garlic
1   (5-ounce) bag spring greens mix
1   head Bibb lettuce, washed and torn
1   head frisée, washed and trimmed
4   medium yellow beets, roasted, peeled, and chopped
1   bunch Broccolini, blanched
½   cup radishes washed, trimmed, and shaved
Shaved Asiago cheese
Garnish: boiled egg wedges

1. Season chicken with salt and pepper.
2. In a small bowl, whisk together vinegar, oil, mustard, tarragon, shallot, and garlic. Place chicken in a large re-sealable plastic bag. Pour half of vinaigrette mixture over chicken. Seal bag, and refrigerate for 2 hours to overnight. Cover and refrigerate remaining vinaigrette.
3. In a large bowl, combine spring mix, Bibb lettuce, frisée, beets, Broccolini, and radishes; toss to combine.
4. Grill chicken over medium-high heat (350° to 400°) for 15 to 20 minutes or until a meat thermometer registers 165°. Let cool for 5 minutes.
5. Slice chicken, and arrange on salad. Drizzle with re-maining vinaigrette; add cheese. Garnish with boiled egg wedges, if desired. Serve immediately.

Bridal Bliss

Vibrant orange and gold set a cheery tone for this gracious gathering. Solid colored tea towels or oversize napkins can be used under a setting in lieu of place mats. Footed bowls and serving pieces make elegant vases for a trailing arrangement, and unique garden-themed place card holders get a color-coordinated update from perky ribbon bows.

MENU

FUZZY NAVEL MIMOSA

MINI HAM AND
MUSHROOM QUICHE

Wedding
BELLES

Raise a toast in tribute to the gracious ladies whose love and loyalty have earned them the title of bridesmaid. With flowers and flourishes, a beautiful brunch showers them with the accolades they deserve.

Mini Ham and Mushroom Quiche
Makes 2 dozen

1   (14.1-ounce) box refrigerated pie crusts
2   tablespoons butter
2   cups finely chopped baby bella mushrooms
½ cup finely chopped onion
½ cup finely chopped red bell pepper
2   teaspoons minced garlic
6   large eggs
1½ cups half-and-half
1   teaspoon dry mustard
¾ teaspoon salt
½ teaspoon ground black pepper
1   cup finely chopped ham
1½ cups finely grated Parmigiano-Reggiano
    cheese, divided

1. Preheat oven to 350°. Spray 2 (12-cup) muffin pans with nonstick cooking spray.
2. On a lightly floured surface, unroll crusts. Using a 3½-inch round cutter, cut 12 circles from each pie crust; reroll scraps as needed. Press crusts into the bottom and up the sides of each cup of muffin pan.
3. In a medium skillet, heat butter over medium-high heat, until butter is melted. Add mushrooms, onion, bell pepper, and garlic. Cook for 6 minutes, or until liquid is evaporated and vegetables are tender; cool completely.
4. In a medium bowl, whisk together eggs, half-and-half, mustard, salt, and pepper until well combined. Evenly divide ham, vegetable mixture, and 1 cup cheese among all prepared crusts. Spoon egg mixture into each crust. Bake for 20 minutes.
5. Remove from oven, and sprinkle tops of quiche with remaining ½ cup cheese; return to oven and bake for 5 minutes. Cool in pans for 5 minutes before removing.

Fuzzy Navel Mimosa
Makes 1 drink

1   ounce fresh orange juice
1   ounce peach nectar
½ ounce peach schnapps
¼ ounce orange-flavored liqueur
4   ounces chilled Champagne
Garnish: orange spiral

1. In a chilled Champagne flute, combine orange juice, peach nectar, peach schnapps, and orange liqueur. Add Champagne. Garnish with orange spiral, if desired.

Beth

Pristine & Soft
White flowers, linens, and china set the tone for a prenuptial celebration. Simple ribbon accents incorporate the bride's chosen color palette into the table setting.

Recipe Index

*"A kind heart is a fountain of gladness,
making everything in its vicinity into smiles."*
—Washington Irving